THE LEADERSHIP
Paradox

THE LEADERSHIP
Paradox

DENNY GUNDERSON

PUBLISHING

A MINISTRY OF YOUTH WITH A MISSION

P.O. Box 55787, Seattle, WA 98155

YWAM Publishing is the publishing ministry of Youth With A Mission. Youth With A Mission (YWAM) is an international missionary organization of Christians from many denominations dedicated to presenting Jesus Christ to this generation. To this end, YWAM has focused its efforts in three main areas: 1) Training and equipping believers for their part in fulfilling the Great Commission (Matthew 28:19). 2) Personal evangelism. 3) Mercy ministry (medical and relief work).

For a free catalog of books and materials write or call:
YWAM Publishing
P.O. Box 55787, Seattle, WA 98155
(425) 771-1153 or (800) 922-2143
www.ywampublishing.com

The Leadership Paradox
Copyright © 1992, 1997 by Denny Gunderson

Second Edition. Updated and expanded.
Formerly titled *Through the Dust.*

10 09 08 07 06 05 04 03 02 01   10 9 8 7 6 5 4 3 2

Published by YWAM Publishing
P.O. Box 55787, Seattle, WA 98155, USA

Unless otherwise noted, Scripture quotations in this book are taken from the Holy Bible, New International Version®, Copyright© 1973, 1978, 1984 by the International Bible Society. Used by permission of Zondervan Publishing House.

ISBN 0-927545-87-X

Printed in the United States of America

To my late father, Carl Gunderson, and my mother, Wilma—loving partners together in over five decades of ministry.

With deep gratitude to...

Dodie, Tanya, and Timmy, my wonderful family, who showed exceeding patience during this project.

Dale Gunderson, my brother, friend, and confidant. Our discussions many years ago on leadership in the Church were the initial spark for this book.

Loren Cunningham, Floyd McClung, Jr., and Leland Paris—my three leaders in Youth With A Mission, all of whom exhibit true servant leadership.

Mr. Tom Marshall from New Zealand, whose wonderful lectures on leadership gave many fresh insights.

Dr. Don Ross, pastor, friend and innovator of new concepts for the local church.

Geoff and Janet Benge, for their helpful advice, inspiration, and encouragement.

Foreword

Denny Gunderson has managed to do two seemingly impossible things at the same time. He has written an unnervingly simple yet deeply profound book that goes beyond your normal how-to leadership book.

This is no manual offering pious platitudes to make your church grow, nor is it a book written to make those of us who struggle with the complexities of leadership have a superficial, feel-good experience.

The values of the Kingdom of God, as fleshed out in the life of Jesus and other biblical biographies, call for a radical response. Denny does not preach at us, he simply tells the stories of Jesus and other biblical figures and applies the lessons contained therein to modern-day leadership paradoxes. His incisive insights cut across leadership dilemmas with profoundly simple yet life-changing lessons.

Denny goes beyond addressing the three classical leadership pitfalls—wealth, women, and glory—and gets to the deeper issues of kingdom core-values and how they are worked out in the life of a servant leader. Though every leader is susceptible to the above-mentioned temptations, a spiritual leader who has not allowed himself to be confronted with the Jesus of the New Testament and

His Kingdom's value system will surely fail. Or to put it in Denny's words from Chapter 4, "The temptation to gain special favor or to extend partial treatment can weave its seductive spell only upon the soul impressed with status."

Denny Gunderson draws upon a wealth of insight through his wide exposure to authors from many parts of the Body of Christ, as well as to those outside the Church. The reader will be challenged to read more about the models those authors present.

Denny probes the issue of personal insecurity being mixed with ministry status and concludes that it is a combustible combination.

This book is a mirror, and in it we can see our own soul. I commend it to every leader who does not want more answers but wants rather to be asking the right questions. I commend Denny Gunderson and the book he has written in a world filled with sham answers and superficial stereotypes. Both Denny and his book are for real.

Floyd McClung, Jr.
All Nations Institute

September 18, 1997

Contents

Prologue

The sand, driven through the air by powerful currents of wind, became tiny projectiles of destruction, exploding upon the helpless caravan. What started as a promising trip to an adjoining city to trade cloth for pottery abruptly became a living hell. The wail of fear emanating from the master's wife spoke for them all. They were helpless in the face of the storm's fury.

"Jehaziel! Jehaziel!" The master attempted to shout over the bellow of the wind. He hated to do it but knew that any hope remaining would soon be snuffed out unless his servant, Jehaziel, attended to duty.

By now, the heaving volumes of dust blocked out the light of the sun. It was almost impossible to breathe. Vertigo was setting in. Man and beast alike were becoming disoriented. All sense of direction was lost.

The servants for the caravan were gasping with the exertion of maintaining order among the animals. The beasts were restless, panicky. If not restrained, they would make a mad dash for shelter and would perish in the desert. In the distant future, Bedouins would stumble across their decomposed bodies.

"Master! Hang on! I'm here!" The words, squeezed from between cracked lips, were barely audible but loud enough to arouse the master from his gruesome reverie.

"Jehaziel? My wife is on behind me. It's up to you. You know I'll reward you handsomely if you get us out of this." The sound of the master's voice was cruelly cut off by the wind's omnipotent force. All the master could do was hold on for dear life, hoping his wife could, too. Their survival now rested solely in the hands of their servant.

It was days later…or was it only hours? The camel groaned, then struggled to its feet. Its burden slid unimpeded to the ground. "Ahhh." The involuntary cry caused the beast's ears to prick up. Slowly, the heap of tangled clothing began to move, then separated as husband and wife rose unsteadily, groping for each other. Tragedy had struck, but at least they were still alive.

Slowly and painfully their swollen eyes attempted to focus. The effort drew tears down their cheeks as vision strained to return. They seemed to be partially shielded to the east by an outcropping of rock.

"We made it!" croaked the man, looking at his wife. She returned his gaze, then glanced inadvertently over his shoulder. An anguished expression came over her face. Turning, the husband followed his wife's line of sight.

"Oh, no!" he cried. Lying half-buried in the sand was the familiar figure of their loyal servant, Jehaziel, his body frozen in the stiff posture of death.

The master and his wife slumped to their knees in silent memorial. It was now apparent that their beloved servant, Jehaziel, had unflinchingly confronted the dust storm. In so doing, he selflessly gave up his own life to save the lives of his master and wife. His sacrifice was rewarded by the humiliation of an inglorious death.

Servanthood Is a Dusty Road

The preceding scenario depicts the origin of the Greek word *servant* used by Jesus when he told the disciples,

"Whoever wants to be great among you must be your servant" (Matthew 20:26). The Greek word used here is *diakonos*. Diakonos consists of two words. *Dia* means "through" or "across," just as *dia*meter is a measurement through the center of a circle. *Konos* may be translated as "dust, dirt, or earth." Thus, diakonos literally means "through the dust." The words *minister* and *deacon* come from this same root. In our story, the diakonos/servant fought his way through the dust storm to sustain the lives of people *other than himself.*

How startling that Jesus chose to use *diakonos* to respond to a request about leadership. On numerous occasions the disciples of Jesus argued among themselves regarding leadership. Their disputes were attended by unrighteous self-interest. The desire for power and position was always the unspoken backdrop for the disciples' remarks. Usually, Jesus refused to dignify their discussion with direct answers, preferring instead to *demonstrate* servanthood. In fact, Jesus had little to say about leadership and even less about how to be a leader. His few references to leaders were primarily negative, leaving one with the impression that he viewed leadership as having secondary importance. Thus, it is little wonder that most contemporary Christian books on leadership shy away from using Jesus as the model for leadership, choosing rather to focus on Moses, David, Nehemiah, or Paul. The relative silence of Jesus regarding leadership, should not, however, be interpreted as meaning that leadership is a nonbiblical concept.

> *What is pomp, rule, reign, but earth and dust.*
>
> —*Shakespeare*

Indeed, the testimony of Scripture is that God has gifted and called people to lead.

What, then, does leadership have to do with servanthood? At first glance these two concepts appear to oppose each other. The Western world today is being inundated with dozens of new books every year on the topics of leadership, management, and vision. Some hint at a revolutionary new approach to this field with the term *servant leadership*, a concept often used manipulatively by suggesting that leaders employ this terminology whether or not they actually practice it. This line of reasoning is that people *want* to believe that their best interests are being served by a well-intentioned, service-oriented salesperson or boss.

In the Church, the same thing often happens. The language of servanthood is used so commonly today that we smile and nod approvingly when we hear it. What is sometimes overlooked is how often the person mouthing the words is not demonstrating them. In some circles where this has been the case, the absence of actions to back up the words has left a weary cynicism.

Another element that complicates this issue is the way in which people interpret what servant leadership means. In one particular venue, a number of people had an expectation that because I had written a book on servant leadership, I would do their work for them! I have also observed leaders who use the term but define it in such a way that they exhibit strong control over their followers. They then defend their control by stating that this is their way of serving people. It is indeed tragic that those who most use the language of servanthood are often the greatest abusers and exploiters of other people.

The point is, people are confused as to the meaning of servant leadership. Part of the reason for this confusion resides in the misconceptions that surround the topic of leadership in general. Another reason for confusion has to do with the paradox intrinsic to the very term *servant leadership*. A paradox exists whenever an assertion *seems* to be self-contradictory. In terms of servant leadership, the word *servant* has a connotation of someone who has no freedom to choose for himself but must do the bidding of a master. By contrast, the word *leader* connotes a person who does the choosing for those whom he leads. Thus many people conclude that a person may be either a servant or a leader but not both simultaneously. Historical observance seems to support this notion. We have all read about leaders, and we have read about servants, but rarely have the two been merged into the same person.

The contention of this book is threefold. First, Jesus Christ is the ultimate model for all leadership models, styles, and concepts. He was and is *the* universal leader. His leadership applies in all cultures and at all times. Second, not only is servant leadership *not* a contradiction of terms, it is the *only* way to properly lead. And third, servant leadership is so radical, so heavenly, we have missed it. My prayer is that this book will give us at least a few clues as to the nature of a leadership style that is eternal.

Dear reader, please bear in mind one important thing as together we look at Jesus' leadership: Jesus never told anyone how to be a leader. Therefore, I certainly cannot tell you how to be one either. All I can do is help you visualize a number of incidents from the

> *Every noble crown is, and on earth will forever be, a crown of thorns.*
>
> —*Thomas Carlyle*

life of Jesus and see whether they apply to us today. In the process, we just might glean a few principles that will help us more clearly point the way to the only Perfect Leader.

CHAPTER ONE

The Control Trap

The test of our spiritual life is the power to descend...
—*Oswald Chambers*

Azor could not deny the hint of expectancy that hung in the air—a restless waiting filled with nervous energy. He had felt it for many months, ever since he had joined John the Baptist. But now, more and more people clustered around John every day, listening intently, yet with the pervading sense that something lingered just beyond their grasp.

As Azor stooped to pick a stone from his sandal, his eyes met those of a small boy whose mother supported him as he hopped along on one leg. The boy's other leg was a swollen, lifeless mass. Azor smiled at them. Two pairs of hopeful eyes stared back at him. Azor understood their plight. Perhaps the Baptist would pray for the young one.

Azor stood and surveyed the crowd. About five hundred people squeezed together on the river's muddy banks. For days now, people had been flocking here to see

John the Baptist. Azor thought back a few months to the first time he had seen John. Something about his spiritual mentor had awakened musty memories of patriarchal figures from a mythical past. It wasn't just his unconventional visage, stern and eccentric as it was. The people were used to such images, having for years observed the studied religiosity of Pharisees, Sadducees, and sundry other would-be holy men.

Perhaps it had been John's eyes, at times flashing with excited ecstasy but more often smoldering with the naked intensity of a person compelled by a long-awaited message. The message itself was so simple: the Messiah was coming. Azor wondered often about this. Would he be one of Abraham's most blessed descendants who would truly see the divine one? What would the Messiah be like? Surely he would be something like the Baptist. And if John could gather such large crowds on his own, how much bigger would the crowds be with the Messiah beside him? What a glorious moment! And according to John, the hour of introduction was nearly upon them.

"He's coming!" trilled the high-pitched voice of a mud-splattered street urchin.

The clusters of people wheeled as one, becoming moblike as they hurriedly vied for vantage points along the riverbank. The cacophonous din of animated voices, yapping dogs, and running feet echoed across the valley.

The determined stride of the Baptist propelled him down the bank and into the stream. For a moment he surveyed the rabble facing him. Then he expelled, "Repent, for the kingdom of God is near."

Some in the crowd were transfixed, while others nudged their neighbors in the ribs, sharing knowing smiles of delight at the audacity of what they were hearing. Something in the air hinted at change, a possible shifting of the established order.

"He will burn up the chaff with unquenchable fire." The words reverberated with detached bluntness.

The throng shifted self-consciously, the preacher's gaze holding their attention though his lips were now silent. No one had ever spoken to them with such certainty and passion. As one of the crowd, Azor could feel the crowd's tension and longing.

Momentarily, Azor became aware of a minor distraction taking place. Quickly, he began to wind his way through the crowd. The hair on the back of his neck raised in warning. What would it be this time? Always at the back of his mind were fears of retaliation by the Roman authorities or trouble being stirred up by the Pharisees. Maybe it would just be the madman bound with ropes who was dragged here daily by his family. Often John said things that disturbed the man, who would become uncontrollable, throwing the weight of his body at those around him.

As Azor approached the center of the distraction, he noticed several of John's other disciples making their way there, too. He made a mental note of their positions, relieved that there were enough of them to deal with any situation.

Surprisingly, the distraction seemed to revolve around a man making his way through the jostling crowd. It wasn't the man himself who was making the commotion. There was nothing unique about his appearance. From a distance, he did not look different from dozens of other similarly aged men sprinkled throughout the crowd of bystanders. He was of average height and wore clothing befitting the common man. He walked purposefully, oblivious to the reactions of those around him. Azor moved into step behind the man, not knowing what to expect.

When at last the stranger came into John's view, a look of recognition flashed between them. "My cousin," breathed the Baptist.

The stranger nodded. "It has been a long time, John. I've come that you might baptize me."

A look of confusion passed across John's face. Never before at a loss for words, John moved his mouth but no words came out. Suddenly, his face went from perplexity to clarity.

"Jesus! You are the one!" It was a statement made more for his own endorsement than for anyone else's. The Baptist spoke with a tone that Azor had never heard him use, a tone of wonder tinged with a trace of shock.

The stranger's eyes locked with John's. Azor felt uneasy. This was not the way others had approached baptism. The Sadducees tended to rip off their tunics and offer long, loud prayers, while many of the women wept or clung to John. As Azor watched, it occurred to him that this stranger and John were playing out some preordained act, each honoring the other as they did so.

It wasn't until later that evening that the Baptist finally spoke to his disciples about the day's bewildering events. Everything had happened so quickly: the voice from the sky, the dove hovering over the stranger's head, the uncharacteristic quiet that came over the normally boisterous crowd. It had been eerie, and as quickly as the stranger had appeared, he disappeared into the dusty landscape. Things seemed normal again, but in his heart, Azor knew that events had somehow changed his mentor forever.

Now for the first time, John was going to speak to them about it. But before he could, one of the group blurted out, "Was that him, the one you have been telling us about?" No one had to articulate who the "him" was, which reminded Azor that this stranger had made an unparalleled impression.

"What was his name? Some people say you are related to him. Is that true?"

John positioned himself on a rock. "Yes. His name is Jesus, and we are related. My mother and his mother are cousins. But I have not seen him for many years, not since we were young boys."

"Does he know who you are?" asked Azor anxiously. "I mean about your miraculous birth and the promise to your parents?" Azor, like many from the region, had heard about Elizabeth's pregnancy late in life and of his father's muteness given as a reminder of his unbelief. Many times John's disciples had bolstered each other's faith with a reminder of the Baptist's unique place in God's sight.

John nodded. "Yes, he knows me. And I know who he is."

"If he is really the one you've told us about, when is he going to begin his reign?" another anxious disciple asked. "Do I have time to return to my village for my sword?"

"Does he want us to wipe out the Romans or merely make Jewish slaves of them?"

"John, he will make you his first in command, won't he? Isn't that part of the plan?"

"Will we get any special privileges because we're your disciples? After all, we have been in this from the beginning."

The questions flew rapidly at John. His disciples were in awe; history and destiny were flowing as one, and they were at the center of it all.

The state of excitement escalated over the next few days and the disciples waited for the inevitable summons. Some became frustrated at the deliberate evasiveness of John. Either he did not know what was going to happen, or he was unwilling to share his knowledge with the group. Either option was very disconcerting.

Almost imperceptibly, a change began taking place. About six weeks after the baptism of Jesus, word reached Azor and the other disciples that Jesus had begun to preach publicly up north. This news rankled Azor, who decided to confront John.

"That man, Jesus, who was with you on the other side of the Jordan. Well, he's preaching up by the Sea of Galilee, and everyone is going to hear him." The statement came tumbling out, a sign of Azor's growing frustration. The implication of his statement was both a challenge and a question: What are you going to do about it?

A bemused but patient look settled upon John's face. "A man can receive only what is given him from heaven." The tone of his voice held no rebuke, just simple instruction. "You yourselves can testify that I once said, 'I am not the Christ, but am sent ahead of him.' I have also said to everyone, 'After me will come one more powerful than I, whose sandal straps I am not worthy to stoop down and untie.'"

John's disciples were now silent. They were captivated by the look of adoration on their leader's face as he spoke.

"The friend who attends the bridegroom waits and listens for him, and is full of joy when he hears the bridegroom's voice. That joy is mine, and it is now complete." John's voice rang with triumph. Some in the small audience were transfixed. Others lingered restlessly, not really understanding.

Then John the Baptist averted his gaze and looked beyond the mortal realm. With a quiet but confident voice he spoke to all mankind and said, "He must increase, but I must decrease."

❧

The human obsession for control and the sincere desire of a true leader to serve are mutually exclusive.

The Test of Fading Influence

Our story of John the Baptist began at a pivotal moment in human history. John was a hero, listened to with respect by the general populace of his day. People traveled great distances to see and hear him. Many even wondered whether he was the promised Messiah. In a very real sense, John was God's man of the hour.

Imagine you were John at the time Jesus came onto the scene. First of all, Jesus was John's cousin. It would be proper to assume that at times as children, John and Jesus had played together. They were peers. When John initially trumpeted the coming of the Messiah, he probably didn't know he was talking about his childhood playmate. What a shock it must have been when John's understanding was opened to see that the Messiah was his cousin. Some Bible commentators have surmised that this revelation took place at the time John baptized Jesus.

Secondly, John was the center of attention in Israel—until Jesus came along. Further, when Jesus began his public ministry, John's crowds became smaller. People shifted allegiance to Jesus. Put yourself in John's shoes. Every day you go to the Jordan River and preach with great passion. But the excitement of large crowds listening with breathless intensity no longer exists. Only a few hangers-on remain.

Let's fast-forward to today. Perhaps you are a spiritual leader, possibly a pastor. You find out that a childhood friend and seminary buddy has moved to your city to start a church a few blocks down the road. How would you feel? What would your inner response be if people in your church left to attend your friend's church? Surely, this is similar to what John faced. In a sense, John initiated his own demise by telling people to follow Jesus rather than himself.

Nothing is more disheartening to the soul of a leader than to be at the pinnacle of fulfillment, the expectancy of grandeur dancing delightedly in his mind, only to be dashed unexpectedly by the realization that he is no longer needed. It is one thing to preach that we are expendable and quite another when the *we* is *me*. I believe it is safe to speculate that this was what John the Baptist experienced. The thrill of knowing that at last the Messiah had arrived was rudely interrupted for John by the reality of dwindling crowds and decreasing influence.

Is Leadership a Position or a Role?

In our day, leadership is defined primarily by formal leadership position, implying that the person having the position has been either hired to be a leader or voted into the position by virtue of his or her leadership gift. The formalization process often brings with it an unwelcome consequence: leaders must have followers. Dare I say that these must become "formal followers"? With this development, two classes now emerge and form into a hierarchical order we label as "over" and "under." "How many people do you have under you?" is a question often asked in leadership gatherings. We ask this in spite of Jesus' declaration that "the rulers of the Gentiles lord it over them, and their high officials exercise authority over them. Not so with you."[1] What does this mean in plain English? I believe that it means *not so with you!* Jesus clearly and unequivocally denounces as worldly any talk or practice that establishes hierarchical orders.

Formalization of position and hierarchies go hand in hand. As Jim Petersen of the Navigators points out, it was some of the Church Fathers two to three hundred years

---

1. Matthew 20: 25-26.

after Christ's life on earth who were responsible for bringing the concept of hierarchy into the Church.

As the Church Fathers attempted to cope with the various pagan philosophies that threatened the church from without and the heresies that were popping up from within, they resorted to establishing a hierarchical structure as their solution. "Hierarchy" comes from two Greek words meaning "rule by priests." Thus, in doing this, our Church Fathers neatly and permanently divided God's people into two castes: laity and clergy. We have lived with this caste system ever since, even though the Bible teaches otherwise.[2]

Once the formalization process is put into motion, the modern-day flowchart is sure to follow. When drawing this chart, the one "over" is usually quick to state that this chart describes only necessary function, not value. Rarely does this prove to be the case, however.

Look at the following chart of a typical denominational structure:

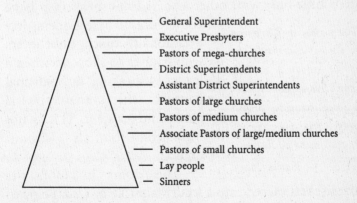

General Superintendent
Executive Presbyters
Pastors of mega-churches
District Superintendents
Assistant District Superintendents
Pastors of large churches
Pastors of medium churches
Associate Pastors of large/medium churches
Pastors of small churches
Lay people
Sinners

---

2. Jim Petersen, *Church Without Walls* (Colorado Springs: NAVPRESS, 1992), p. 165.

Here is an obvious question: To whom do we accord the most respect? Isn't it usually to the person with the most people *under* him/her, in this case the General Superintendent? This does, in fact, become a way of conferring value. When people exchange business cards, they often look at the person's title before they notice the person's name. Why is this? Isn't it because they want to know how much respect to give this person or how much influence the person possesses? In most formal organizational settings, when the "top" person walks into the room, the followers seem to change personalities. As the leader mixes with the crowd, the people exchange their normal appearance for one that is more beatific, usually accompanied by a smile. This is not necessarily the leader's fault, but it does point out the silliness of man's value systems.

I believe it's proper to ask another question: If Jesus were walking on earth today in a human body, who on this chart would he spend the most time with? The answer is too obvious for me to state. Yet, during my lifetime in the body of Christ I have observed leaders who spend their time only with other leaders or as speakers at large conferences. These leaders may occasionally touch unbelievers who happen to show up when a leader is speaking, but personal contact with unbelievers is almost nonexistent. This is not only ironic but also without excuse.

> *The pastor or Christian leader who is constantly the object of adoring crowds soon can't live without it and, often unconsciously, begins to shape his message to assure continued adulation.*
>
> —*Charles Colson*

The point is, John the Baptist was placed into a leadership role *by God*. Being in a prophetic role, John had the primary responsibility to simply minister according to his calling. He knew his role, but I'm convinced he was oblivious to our modern-day concept of leadership.

By every measure, John was a true servant leader. His greatest desire was simply to minister. That sounds so obvious, but many today want to start or lead ministries more than they want to minister. When ministry (noun) takes priority over minister (verb), servanthood is squeezed out.

Over the years I have had occasion to serve on many different ministry boards. Some of these ministries seemed to be focused more on perpetuating their ministry (as an organization) than on actually ministering. When talking to the leaders of these organizations, one can't help but notice how much conversation is dominated by talk of fundraising, growth projections, administrative troubleshooting, and public image. To be sure, it is not wrong to talk about these subjects. However, when these are the *primary* topics, and sometimes the sole topics, something is off track. In one of these settings I once told a leader that he needed to spend more time ministering and less time endeavoring to start a ministry (admittedly, I was a bit frustrated). Once the noun *ministry* rather than the verb *to minister* is emphasized, the dreary inevitability exists that formal leadership positions must be quickly forthcoming.[3]

The Perpetuity Myth

The example of John the Baptist points out another attitude of the servant leader. John's public ministry lasted only six months, followed by nine months in prison, at

---

3. Please understand me. I am not saying that it is *wrong* to have formal positions and organizational flow-charts. I *am* saying that when these become the dominating themes within a local church or para-church ministry, the perpetuation of the ministry often takes precedence over ministering.

which point John was beheaded. Think of it: thirty years of preparation for only six months of public ministry!

An unspoken assumption often resides in the mind of a leader chosen by God to lead a church or other ministry. In my own mind, it goes something like this: "Because God called me to a leadership position, this is my calling for life. Not only am I called to this position, but the ministry I am leading should exist forever. After all, it was a calling from God."

Let me be blunt. This type of reasoning, of which I have been guilty, is fraught with the danger of self-interest. Our fleshly side wants to perpetuate the importance of our position. In my case, I would have protested with proper spiritual-sounding jargon that "the ministry belongs to God," while internally seeking to justify the assurance of my position within "God's ministry."

In the 1980s a ministry that I had started reached a wonderful peak of effectiveness. But then, at about our seventh year of existence, we began to lose momentum. I recall the distinct agony of literally watching the disintegration of this ministry that I felt I had birthed. Funds began to dry up. The enrollment of our training schools began to drop, and the morale of my eighty staff members (I really did believe they were *my* staff even though they were all volunteers) began to plummet.

Half the harm that is done in this world is due to people who want to feel important.

—T.S. Eliot

At first, I responded by attempting to rally the troops, informing them that we were being attacked by the enemy (there is probably always some truth in that thinking). Eventually, however, the sad realization began to dawn upon me that regardless of other mitigating factors, God was putting his finger on one of my Achilles heels: the need to be in charge. My identity was wrapped in my position as a leader. As a result, my carnal side was bombarding me with the unwelcome notion that if the ministry failed, my reputation and standing as a leader would be irreparably damaged.

Finally, after eighteen months of personal struggle, a few of the remaining leaders and I decided it was time to allow the ministry to die! We suggested to our staff members that they seek guidance from the Lord as to where they should go. This was not a case of abdicating our responsibility or of seeking to cover up our failure. Rather, it was an honest attempt to face the uncomfortable reality that decay had come into a once-thriving ministry. As the primary leader, I had to embrace failure and come to grips with a side of myself that I did not want to see. By the way, embracing one's own failure and expendability is a major step of liberation away from the bondage of self-interest.

The Fear of Failure

M. Scott Peck points out, "The need for control—to ensure the desired outcome—is at least partially rooted in the fear of failure."[4] Often, our ambition to lead may indicate a lifelong pattern of covering up our need to control. Possessing a leadership position may grant us the feeling of importance that our fragile sense of self-worth so desperately seeks. Within my own heart, I was constantly looking for ways to validate my leadership position. And if threatened in my role, it was easy to move from a defensive posture to one of aggression. Therefore, the thought of failing as a leader was absolutely abhorrent. The result for me was bondage to performance-oriented ministry, a most cruel and exacting taskmaster.

4. M. Scott Peck, *The Different Drum* (New York: Simon and Schuster, 1987), p. 99.

I am not suggesting that to be a servant leader one should arbitrarily and repeatedly abdicate a God-given role of leadership. I am suggesting, however, that there should be a constant willingness to step aside should God indicate the wisdom in doing so. This may require the relinquishment of a prized position, leaving the security of a solid financial "power base," or voluntarily minimizing one's own importance so that someone else can have an opportunity to rise to a place of prominence.

The true servant leader, with nothing to prove and no vested interest, takes joy in seeing others grow *beyond* himself. In the words of Henri Nouwen, "The beginning and the end of all Christian leadership is to give your life for others."[5] Jesus said it even better. "The Son of Man did not come to be served, but to serve, and to give his life as a ransom for many" (Matthew 20:28). In other words, servant leadership simply means that we give our lives away.

The sovereignty of God makes no allowance for accidents. It is surely not accidental that Jesus' public ministry was heralded by one whose own ministry began to quietly recede into the gray background of relative unimportance. Theoretical ministry concepts and the stark reality of God's will often collide at this point. Could it be God is actually looking for leaders who are willing to lead by knowing when to take a back seat? Is it possible that a living demonstration of selflessness could make a greater contribution to promoting New Testament leadership values than our eloquent verbiage and natural gifts for decisive action?

Planned Obsolescence?

I have heard for years that one of the goals of a leader is to work himself out of a job. I agree. A commitment to

---

5. Henri J.M. Nouwen, *The Wounded Healer* (Image Books, 1979), p. 71.

planned obsolescence may produce inferior automobiles, but it makes for great servant leaders. Of course, true servants by their very nature can never be truly obsolete. In reality, the growth of godly influence spreads exponentially in proportion to one's willingness to *not* be recognized and rewarded. Are you willing to walk this narrow path, knowing it could mean the relinquishment of your dreams of fame, glory, and ego fulfillment?

God, in His sovereign wisdom, allows spiritual leaders to be repeatedly tested on the point of leadership identity. Simply stated, the test is this: Are we willing to embrace God's will even when His will appears to hold a deterioration of our personal place of importance as a leader? Is our identity so wrapped up in our leadership position that the loss of position causes us deep emotional trauma? Can we make John the Baptist's choice to decrease?

For Personal Study

1. How have I felt inside when someone I know has been chosen for a position I wanted? Did I resent the person or belittle him?

2. Do I respond to people in positions of leadership differently than I respond to other people?

3. In leadership positions I have held, how did my position affect me? How did I affect those I was leading?

4. Scott Peck stated that "the need for control...is at least partially rooted in the fear of failure." Has the fear of failure caused me to try to exert undue control over others? In what ways?

For Group Discussion

1. Are flowcharts a necessary evil, and, if so, how can we ensure that they describe only function and not value?

2. Discuss some examples of leaders who have willingly set aside their positions for the good of the ministries or organizations they were serving.

3. Why are the obsession for control and the desire to serve mutually exclusive?

4. What are the implications of the statement, "One of the goals of a leader is to work himself out of a job"?

CHAPTER TWO

The Siren Call of Stardom

We prefer a tall, handsome, and, above all, slender Jesus.
—Philip Yancey

When battling insomnia, Simon usually would have gone to the back of the house and climbed the stairs to the roof. He had spent many nights up there, staring out over the city. Capernaum was never completely quiet, often mimicking his own restless spirit. But tonight was different.

There was no way he could mount the stairs. If he were to step outside his mother-in-law's door, he could be barraged by more questions. It was impossible to say from looking out the west window, but he guessed there must be at least three hundred people sprawled out across the street. Some were sitting on bed rolls. The temple beggars were there. A small child began to cry and was quicky silenced at his mother's breast. Many of the neighborhood men were crouched in small groups, talking in excited tones.

Simon knew exactly how they felt. Although he had been traveling with the Master for several weeks, nothing had prepared him for this day. It was too mind-boggling, too overwhelming to take in. He thought back to how he had come to be involved with Jesus.

He and three others had felt a glowing sense of calm and purpose about Jesus. And when he said to them, "Follow me and I will make you fishers of men," to Simon it had seemed the only right thing to do. None of them knew exactly what a "fisher of men" was. It didn't really matter at the time.

But this...today...went beyond anything Simon could have imagined. Simon thought back over the morning's events. The Master stood in the synagogue to teach. He taught in the same way he called them to follow him: with authority and certainty. How different from other religious leaders who had the unique ability to say nothing in ten different ways!

With all the attention the Master attracted, nobody noticed Galal, the maniac, slip in. Simon's mother-in-law told Simon that it took several men to calm Galal down once he got started and that the Pharisees banned him from being in the synagogue at all.

Just when Jesus was reaching the climactic point of his sermon, Galal began one of his screaming tirades. "Why are you here, Jesus of Nazareth? Have you come to destroy us all?" Simon was standing near, and he watched the Master's reactions closely. Without fear or even irritation, the Master looked over at Galal and with magesterial calm said, "Be silent and come out of him."

Galal's body contorted, and he fell to the ground as if twisted by some great invisible hand. After a blood-chilling scream and some whimpering, Galal became silent.

Jesus continued his message. Finally, Galal raised his head and looked around as if just awakening from a deep sleep. And then he smiled…peacefully. The Master looked deeply into his eyes, acknowledging Galal's smile before continuing to read from Isaiah's scroll.

Simon scarcely heard another word as the Master read on. Just who was this man they were following? What would he do next? And, more to the point, what would he require of them if they stayed with him? Simon's imagination had already been stretched so much he wasn't sure he could absorb more.

Simon slipped out to ask his mother-in-law whether they could lodge at her house, only to find her very ill with a high fever. Her eyes were sunken, and her clothes were soaked and smelly with perspiration. Simon had no idea how long she had lain there alone, but there was no more water in the jar, nor was there bread to eat.

Without hesitation, Simon ran back and pushed through the crowd to summon Jesus. The Master followed Simon into the house. Seeing the woman's condition, Jesus reached down and gently took her hand, holding it in his own. No words came from his mouth, but those in the room were silenced by the fierce look of concentration on the Master's face. Simon's mother-in-law opened her eyes and fixed them upon Jesus for several moments. Then, still holding Jesus' hand, she sat up and swung her legs over the side of the bed. Jesus smiled and asked, "Feeling better?"

As the day turned into evening, the news of the Master's ministry spread rapidly. A steady stream of sick, diseased, and possessed people were brought to the little house. The street out front began to take on a carnival-like atmosphere. That evening the power of God was displayed in ways never before seen by the inhabitants of Capernaum. Even those who knew the ancient Scriptures well could not recall an instance when anything of this magnitude happened in their forefathers' day. By the end of the day, hardly a person in the city was left unaffected by the ministry of Jesus.

And now, with the sun set behind the western hills, it seemed the entire town was gathered around the house of Simon's mother-in-law. No wonder Simon couldn't settle down. There was so much planning to be done. The Master seemed very vague when it came to handling the crowds. At one point, the crowd almost went out of control. The Master didn't seem to notice. Simon therefore reasoned that it might be best if he got things a bit more organized. Capernaum would make a good place for ministry headquarters. Set on the edge of the Sea of Galilee, it was the commercial and social center for the surrounding area. The Master had certainly made a deep impression on the city. His actions in the synagogue had shown his great power to the priests as well as to the common people.

Simon cradled his head in his large hands as he mulled over the implications of the day's events. Sleep was far from him.

It was well before dawn when the Master arose from his bed. Glancing out the window, he tied his bedroll together. Then he strode to where Simon was sitting against a wall.

"Hand me your cloak, Simon, so people don't recognize me. I need to go alone and be with my Father."

Simon looked up, startled. "Certainly, Rabbi," he said, handing over his cloak.

The Master wrapped the large black garment tightly around himself and raised the hood over his head. "When you have need of it, you may take mine," he said to Simon, gesturing toward the gray cloak by the door. Then he quietly unlatched the door and slipped unnoticed into the darkness.

Morning finally arrived. Even with a minimal amount of sleep Simon felt energized by the need to organize this new and exciting day. Outside, the crowd was beginning to chant the Master's name, calling for him to come out and minister to them.

Some of those with infirmities became agitated when Jesus did not emerge from the house. Simon empathized with them. And where was the Master? There was so much for him to do—demons to be cast out, the sick to be healed.

James and John inquired as to the Master's whereabouts. "You mean you let the Rabbi go out alone?" James chastised Simon when he heard that the Master had left well before dawn.

"How was I to know he wouldn't be back by now?" Simon countered. "What did you expect me to do? Hold him here?"

John, seeing the rise of explosive tempers, offered a solution. "We could go and get him now. Perhaps he is already conducting a meeting down by the marketplace.

"I'll go," offered Simon. "I let the Master go off alone, so I will bring him back."

It took longer than expected before Simon found Jesus. In fact, if he hadn't recognized his own cloak, Simon probably would not have even stopped to see whether the man sitting under the olive tree was the Master. "Come on, we have to get back," Simon urged. His face was animated by a flush of relief and excitement. "Everyone is looking for you."

Instead of responding with similar excitement at the realization that he had stayed too long, the Master motioned for Simon to sit down.

"It is time for us to go on to the next town, Simon. I must preach in many places, for that is the reason I came."

Simon looked astounded. Jesus appeared so serene. "What's going on," Simon thought to himself. Every door of opportunity was already open in Capernaum. Why not stay? There would be plenty of time to visit other cities later.

The Master rose and began walking in a southerly direction toward Gennesaret. Simon did not know whether to go back and get the others or stay with the Master. How could Jesus be doing this? What more could he want? Simon grimaced at the thought that his mother-in-law was expecting them for breakfast and that there were all manner of needy people waiting to talk with the Master and see him perform miracles.

Simon vascillated for a moment, but then grudgingly fell into step behind Jesus. How would he explain the Master's behavior? What was it the Master really wanted? It had all fit so perfectly into place yesterday, but now it was just the two of them trudging unrecognized through an olive grove.

———⚬⚬⚬———

Obedience and humility are God's twin guardians against the plague of vain ambition resident within the heart of the leader who wants to be a star.

The Cult of Celebrity

The writer of Hebrews says, "For we do not have a high priest who is unable to sympathize with our weaknesses, but we have one who has been tempted in every way, just as we are—yet without sin" (Hebrews 4:15). How often we use this verse—and properly so—to help ward off the temptation toward the external sins of lying, cheating and adultery. But the secret sins of envy, covetousness, jealousy, and sheer egomania more often work their seductive magic upon the heart. Even Jesus must have been tempted in these hidden areas.

Imagine the festive atmosphere that first day in Capernaum. Place yourself on the scene and into the role of Jesus. Literally everyone is talking about you and your remarkable powers. You have just attracted an entire city by your ministry. You have performed startling miracles and stand at the center of activity. What a wonderful opportunity it would be to go from anonymous carpenter to full-fledged celebrity in one step.

You and I might reason that because God's anointing and favor were obviously shining down on us, it would only be appropriate to seize the moment. We would want to exploit any good thing that happens in our ministry and turn it into a public relations bonanza. This desire can often be accompanied by the not so subtle hint that our ministry is the only one really doing the job. Therefore, we can be so bold as to demand, *in Jesus name*, financial support.

Jesus refused to submit to conventional wisdom at this point. On numerous occasions he even told people *not* to tell others how they had been healed. Didn't Jesus understand that he was bypassing wonderful opportunities to build his ministry? Was he so ignorant of financial realities that he failed to properly take advantage of his ministry prowess as the Son of God? Shouldn't he have hired people to get the word out that revival was taking place?

The disciples, on the other hand, were dazzled by their master's exploits and would have stopped at nothing to feed the machinery of publicity. You and I would probably have done the same. As members of the Church, we who inhabit the Western world have been seduced by the pragmatic efficiency of the world's system. It is indeed difficult to argue with a system that works, delivering on its promise to produce results that satisfy the three pillars of success in America—size, speed, and public exposure. In our anxious desire to validate the fruit of our ministries, we give in to this unholy trinity. We justify methods that do a tragic disservice to Jesus, the very one in whose name we are ministering. Newsletters are packed with unembarrassed paeans to our own ministries. Blatant and self-serving stories are told in order to "release" money. Entire pages are filled in an attempt to convince readers of the strategic role our ministry plays in the evangelical pantheon.

Lewis Lapham, essayist and editor of *Harper's Magazine*, speaks of the cult of celebrity to which America is drawn. I believe his comments apply not just to Hollywood and Washington, D.C. but also to the Church. Lapham details how, beginning in the 1960s, the lines between fact and fiction in our publications became increasingly blurred:

> The previously distinct genres of journalism, literature, and theater gradually fused into something known as media. The amalgam of forms resulted in a national theater of celebrity…If the media succeed with their spectacles and grand simplifications, it is because their audiences define happiness as the state of being well and artfully deceived.[1]

> *From the beginning of his ministry, Jesus charged those who experienced his power to say nothing about it.*
>
> *—Walter Wangerin, Jr.*

I wish there were a gentle way to say this: Ministries who *Christianize* self-serving publications to attract donors are no better than the media at large that Lewis Lapham rightfully skewers. By Christianize I mean we use the same self-glorifying methods used by the world but embellish our stories with evangelically accepted jargon. The line of separation between truth and fantasy

1. Lewis H. Lapham, *Imperial Masquerade* (New York: Grove Weidenfeld, 1990), pp. 13-14.

vanishes into something called "testimony" or "vision." Generally speaking, this works because people *want* to have larger-than-life heroes. These exaggerated claims are rationalized on the grounds that the end justifies the means.

Doorways of opportunity can quickly become trap doors for the leader driven to promote his ministry. The enticement of success and popularity can easily delude a leader into believing the fallacy that opportunity and guidance are synonymous. Add to this the clamoring expectations of followers, and an almost irresistible pull develops that can easily lure a leader away from accomplishing the true will of God. It is naive to assume that just because a person is a Christian leader, he is filled with a boundless reservoir of virtue that will prohibit him from ever being deceived.

The "Always" Principle

I am certain Jesus faced the temptation to sell out to fast results. Yet it seems he was almost oblivious to ministry momentum, not because of anything he said, but by his refusal to capitalize on the situations and opportunties created.

Why was this? What force exerted itself in Jesus' life that pulled him away from the temptation to sell out? By extension, we understand that this same force can save us from falling into the pit of materialism and showmanship rather than pursuing servant leadership. The answer is simple. One

> The great masses of the people...will more easily fall victims to a big lie than to a small one.
>
> —Adolph Hitler

principle alone guided Jesus' response to any situation: "The one who sent me is with me; he has not left me alone, for I *always* do what pleases him" (John 8:29). By putting the Father's will above his own, Jesus dwelt in that serene place where ego, prestige, and position had no dominion. He was resolutely single-minded and had only one agenda: to fulfill the will of his Father, *always*.

Each of us must ask the Holy Spirit to search our heart and reveal to us those things we are doing, often in Jesus' name, that are not in accordance with God's guidance for our life. Constrained by love for Jesus, we must seek to order everything in accordance with his will, even if it means forfeiting wonderful opportunities to further enhance our leadership standing. We must have the courage and conviction to say no to a coveted opening, even when knowing that by doing so another leader may take our place in reaping the rewards.

Why do we find it so hard to emulate Jesus' leadership style in this regard? A cursory glance over the past decade of "Christian" headlines is enough to convince even the most rabid evangelical that leaders often do put aside their calling to play the "Gain and Fame Game." Although no leader whom I have met would ever admit to having a desire to become a celebrity, the posturing and self-generated media hype surrounding some leaders in the body of Christ make some celebrity superstars look humble. Hyperbole and hoopla are cheap substitutes for the reality of the Holy Spirit's gentle, unobtrusive presence.

Rejecting the True Model

I believe we frequently reject the Jesus model of leadership for a number of reasons. First, the nature of true servant leadership goes deeply against the grain of human ego. In our current sophistication, we have mastered the abilities of cover-up and spiritualization to such a degree that we offer mere lip service to the possibility of pride while denying its insidious work in our hearts. We tend to view others as being proud of their positions or abilities while carefully crafting our own public personas that place us at the apex of Christian endeavor. Is no one embarrassed by the competing claims to be on the cutting edge of what God is currently doing? How many Cutting Edge Ministries can there really be? Can one be a self-proclaimed Cutting Edger and servant leader at the same time?

It is easy to speak the language of servanthood. Indeed, it is currently in vogue to do so. Phrases such as "I just want to serve" and "I just want to be a nobody for Jesus" are spoken with smooth piety in countless sermons and speeches. Watch out for the nobodies! If one has to say it, he is probably not doing it. Hidden agendas are usually cloaked in enticing dialects. It is quite possible to attain a little self-glory by strategically placed evangelical vernacular, but there is no glamour in the hidden work of service.

A second reason we often miss Jesus' way of leadership is that our concentration on an American-style success ethos fuels us with a tainted incentive to look good at all costs. Working feverishly, we sacrifice the future to look good today. We make promises and announce big plans that will never come about, but we look and sound successful. When challenged on such issues, we wax eloquent on the nature and calling of visionary leadership while our followers clamor for more vision-talk.

A close friend and I were once involved in facetious dialogue about how easy it is to impress people. Our conclusion was that as long as you prattle on about grand schemes and visions, people will tend to view you as successful. In America, appearance counts more than reality. We even have books that instruct us how to dress to look successful, the implication being that as long as you *look* like a winner, the actuality is superfluous. How else do you explain that seventy percent of the people who wear jogging shoes never jog!

A third reason we reject the Jesus model of leadership is our current obsession with packaging. By that I mean we want a formula or technique, able to be easily duplicated, that we herald as The Key to leadership (or success, or power, or the miraculous). We then insert The Key (which we say came by divine revelation or from the Bible) into a catchy slogan and start a movement, complete with teaching tapes, bookmarks, bumper stickers, and cable TV programs. Is advertising or the use of current technology wrong? Of course not. What *is* wrong is the man-centered, self-glorifying, ego-inflating packaging that we have come to accept as a normal part of modern Christendom.

Is it proper, then, for the potential leader to have a sense of destiny or ambition? The answer is a qualified yes, if one understands destiny to mean God-ordained calling and direction. One's destiny can become one's test, however. The individual driven to act out and prove that he or she is a special chosen vessel can easily forfeit the anointing to lead. The initial calling may well have been from God, but unchecked ego will pervert the call. Vain ambition disguises itself with assertions of uniqueness. Destiny bound to ego easily degenerates into empire building, and empire builders have the unfortunate tendency to become false prophets.

> One of the blunders religious people are particularly fond of making is the attempt to be more spiritual than God.
>
> —Frederick Buechner

The leader wishing to emulate Jesus resists the great temptation to build a ministry around himself. He chooses to abandon himself to the will and pleasure of God on a moment-by-moment basis. Thus, communion takes precedence over causes, and obedience over opportunity. Leadership pleasing to God is reserved for those servants willing to enter the crucible of divine dictate, often forfeiting opportunities for advancement in the process.

The Deceitful Heart

The Bible is much more realistic than we are about the human condition. The prophet Jeremiah informs us, "The heart is deceitful above all things and beyond cure. Who can understand it?" (Jeremiah 17:9) After dealing with my own deceitfulness for many years, I can recognize telltale signs when my own motives are not right. Let me outline five of the most basic:

1. **Status**. Status has to do with privilege. It is characterized by special titles and rewards by virtue of position or standing. Status is one of the most seductive elements inherent in a leadership position. Those who are addicted to the expectation of preferential treatment because of their position have already been seduced by the magnetism of status.

2. **Name dropping**. A person with the compulsion to inform others of such things as the important invitations he receives or the famous people he knows is deeply insecure. His insecurity will cloud his motives.

> The imposter does not want to come out of hiding. He will grab for the cosmetic kit and put on his pretty face to make himself "presentable."
>
> —Brennan Manning

3. **Defensiveness**. Defensiveness is the twin of arrogance. Arrogance may be defined as the unwillingness to be corrected or checked. The person who closes himself off from reproof is determined to run things according to personal desire. He will end up surrounding himself with those who, blindly loyal, only affirm his ideas and decisions.

4. **Self-promotion**. Vain ambition is at the heart of the need to promote one's own ministry. For the leader beset by this motive, people become pawns or contacts who are used to further the leader's credibility or reputation. Using people in this way is not always a conscious act, but it will undoubtedly surface when one is frantically scrambling to establish a ministry upon the sifting sand of human effort.

5. **Using the end to justify the means**. Compromising ethical integrity starts out as just a "small" thing, especially in fiscal matters. Rationalizing the need to get the message out, the leader suppresses the still, small voice of conscience to keep the ministry going.

For Jesus, Capernaum represented a prime opportunity to start his ministry. One of the greatest tests for any aspiring servant leader is to walk away from Capernaum as Jesus did. Can we follow his example? Are the hooks of ambition and status too firmly embedded in us? Let our eyes be fixed on Gennesaret and the villages beyond, lest we become entangled in our Capernaums, unable to disentangle ourselves to do the will of Jesus.

For Personal Study

1. In the secret places of my own heart, do I fantasize about being a "star"? Would I like to be a famous Christian?

2. How has my ego responded to awards I've been given or positions I've been voted into? How has God dealt with me regarding my ego?

3. In situations of my past, when have I been affected by a desire for status? Do I secretly enjoy having status conferred upon me?

4. What evidence is there to suggest that my serving has been either (a) self-serving, or (b) God-pleasing? Am I quick to serve, or do I avoid serving?

For Group Discussion

1. How has the concept of "celebrity" affected the modern day Church?

2. Read Mark 1:21-38 together. In what ways does Jesus display humility and obedience to the Father?

3. In the above scriptures, did Jesus meet every need that existed in Capernaum? If not, why do you think He left the city?

4. "Doorways of opportunity can quickly become trap doors for the leader driven to promote his ministry." What does this mean? What are some possible trap doors?

CHAPTER THREE

Transformed by Acceptance

*The most healing thing that we can do with someone
who is in pain, rather than trying to get rid of that
pain, is to sit there and be willing to share it.*
—M. Scott Peck

Nehu hoisted Ezra onto his shoulders. "Can you see
now?" he asked, raising his voice above the din of
the swelling crowd.

"No, Papa. That fig tree is still in the way," Ezra replied.

Nehu wondered what he should do next. Actually, he
would have liked to continue with his work, but that was
impossible. He could not understand what all the fuss was
about. So a holy man was coming to town! Holy men were
always coming to town. But Nehu had never before had to
close his booth because of it. He'd heard snippets of information all morning. This holy man apparently could perform miracles. And even though he wasn't actually a priest
or a rabbi, he often read and taught in synagogues.

Nehu let out a sigh of frustration. Why didn't the man
just come to town on the Sabbath? Today was a busy day
in the market. Finally, Nehu had no choice but to close his

booth. The gathering crowd had been packed so tightly in front of the booth that it had been pointless trying to sell any more cloth. And besides, the crowd wanted nothing from any merchant this afternoon. They were waiting expectantly for the holy man.

As Nehu turned to move farther down the road, he caught sight of the tax collector. Zacchaeus stood out because he was shorter and wider than anyone else and his apparel was gaudy. Several conspicuous rings glistened on Zacchaeus' fingers. The expensive brocade robe encompassing the tax collector's girth accentuated his stubby bulk. Nehu knew the robe was expensive because it had come from the most exquisite bolt in his stall. He cursed the fact that he had not seen Zacchaeus coming in that day in time to hide his most expensive merchandise. Naturally, Zacchaeus wanted the fabric. It became obvious he was not going to leave until he had been "given" a robe's length of the fabric.

Nehu swore to himself. Was nothing safe anymore? The Romans had done more than rule over the Jews. They had subverted them—Jew against Jew, one man's wits against the next. Even some within one's own household were willing to be informers, ready to do the overlord's bidding for small enough reward.

The corners of Nehu's lips curled as he watched Zacchaeus. Perhaps standing too long in the afternoon sun had made the crowd overly bold. It seemed to Nehu that some form of collective drunkenness had come over them as they crudely jostled Zacchaeus.

Normally, none of them would have dared touch the chief tax collector, but now one person nudged him with his elbow while the next person stuck his foot out to trip him. The crowd would never let Zacchaeus get to any kind of vantage point even remotely suiting either the man's diminutive height or his ego.

Nehu broke into a broad grin as he watched the scene. This was worth half a day's business to see. Finally, the tax collector retreated in exasperation, a glare fixed on his face.

The pantomime over, Nehu slipped the small child off his shoulder. "We might as well go farther down the road. The whole town seems transfixed with this man's arrival." They moved along behind the crowd. The heat from the noonday sun intensified. The gentle breeze blowing earlier had disappeared, and now the dust kicked up by the crowd hung like a blanket in the sweltering air.

Nehu selected a spot under the shade of a huge sycamore tree from which to view the arrival of the holy man. He hoisted his son onto his shoulders and waited. This man must surely be important, Nehu speculated, as he spotted numerous men of status from the village among the crowd.

Suddenly the crowd erupted. Nehu craned his neck to see over the two women in front of him. The holy man was coming closer. He made his way slowly, stopping now and then to speak with people. Nehu was too far away to hear what was being said, but there was no hiding the fact that this man was enormously popular. As the holy man drew closer, the sense of excitement in the air captivated Nehu. He found himself anxious to get a good look at the man.

It was as though someone had read his thoughts. The holy man stopped directly in front of Nehu, whose heart skipped a beat. The man looked into Nehu's eyes for a moment. His eyes were warm and dark and held neither malice nor fear. Nehu felt strangely naked and vulnerable. Then the holy man's gaze shifted to the branches of the tree above Nehu.

"Zacchaeus!"

Nehu turned his head to follow the holy man's gaze. Then he saw Zacchaeus clutching unceremoniously and desperately to one of the lower branches. Nehu was incredulous. Did Zacchaeus have no dignity at all? And how did this stranger know Zacchaeus' name? Maybe he knew of the tax collector's disgusting reputation.

For the second time that day, Nehu waited to see the fat little man publicly humiliated. This time it was not merely the jostling of a few street merchants. It was the visiting celebrity himself who was going to address the pompous Roman sellout. Again Nehu smiled. He saw it all. This holy man was a brilliant strategist. He had obviously asked someone to go ahead to find out who was the most unpopular person in town. By publicly denouncing that person he would win over many people instantly. Nehu waited expectantly.

The holy man spoke. "Zacchaeus, hurry and come down from your tree. I need to stay at your house tonight."

A murmur of disbelief rippled through the crowd. People looked at the stranger, then at Zacchaeus, searching for meaning in the absurd request. The holy man and the tax collector? How could this be? Most of the townspeople looked disappointed. One even grumbled, "If he's such a spiritual giant, how could he even acknowledge the existence of the fat tax man?" Those who heard muttered their assent.

Quickly, and with surprising agility considering his size, the chief tax collector climbed down from the tree. The crowd parted as the two men moved toward each other. A genuine smile of friendship spread across the holy man's face as he embraced the rotund figure of Zacchaeus.

Then, unexpectedly, as much as anything could be unexpected at that moment, the tax collector blurted out, "Lord! Here and now I give half of my possessions to the poor, and if I have cheated anybody out of anything, I will pay back four times the amount."

Nehu watched, spellbound, hardly aware of the small

child on his shoulders tugging at his hair to get down. Could the tax collector really mean this? What was going on here? Was the holy man really going to defile himself by staying with a traitor? And was Zacchaeus really serious about what he had just said, or had he become deranged?

There was genuine warmth in the stranger's face as he spoke respectfully with the tax collector. Or was he really speaking to the crowd? "Today salvation has come to this house, because this man too, is a son of Abraham. For the son of man came to seek and to save what was lost."

Like most of the others, Nehu was still trying to grasp this totally unexpected development when Zacchaeus brushed past him. "Yours will be the first booth I stop at tomorrow. I have a debt to settle. I believe this cloth was very expensive. I shall bring my purse with me." Zacchaeus smiled a simple, transparent smile, completely lacking in guile as far as Nehu could tell.

Somehow as he watched the two men make their way down the crowded street, Nehu really believed Zacchaeus would be at his booth tomorrow—but not the same Zacchaeus he had known before.

The servant leader seeks to help others grow, not by attempting to straighten them out, but by establishing a relational base of love and acceptance. The attribute of acceptance emanating from the leader often becomes the sole means of rescue for the despised, rejected, and hopeless people of the world.

The Need to Belong

All human beings have a need to belong. Those who have not found their acceptance needs met in a family or group setting will suffer from a sense of abandonment. Abandonment in turn produces the widespread curse of shame that holds so many people in its grip. Shame-based individuals are driven by their shame to find a place of safety. Unfortunately, shame has a built-in distortion factor that predisposes people to repeatedly fail in their attempt to find safety. Young people from dysfunctional families who join street gangs are an example of this phenomenon. Ironically, these youth find a degree of acceptance within the gang, but it's a conditional acceptance that lasts only as long as the individual stays in a codependent relationship of conformity to the gang.

Temperament also enters as a response factor. Typically, introverts will isolate themselves to prevent continued hurt. Extroverts, on the other hand, will often become aggressive and obnoxious, endeavoring to cover up their feelings of rejection with an I-don't-care-what-you-think attitude.

Zacchaeus falls into the latter category. He was the most despised person in the small city of Jericho. Under the surface of his harsh, pushy demeanor existed a deeply wounded and rejected person. Zacchaeus gloried in his position as *chief* tax collector. But his ostentatious display of wealth and importance was an attempt to hide the fact that he had no identity as a *person*. Zacchaeus' sole identity was found in his *position*. Position and power were props with which he attempted to confront a life with no joy and a bleak future.

> *Character is what you are in the dark.*
>
> —D.L. Moody

Besides having a major self-image problem, Zacchaeus was deficient in character. Human character is primarily a product of choices and decisions. Zacchaeus habitually stole and extorted money from the people. He thought only of himself. He made wrong choices. It would be logical to assume that people's feelings toward Zacchaeus were a combination of fear and loathing.

How unlikely (from a human standpoint) then, that Jesus would single out Zacchaeus, not for rebuke and correction but for fellowship. Of course, Jesus singles out *all of us* who are weak in character and filled with shame. Isn't it likely that Jesus seeks to establish relationship with us because of the potential for good he sees in us rather than the actuality of our sinfulness? If this is the case, should not we as leaders do the same?

The Leader with No Congregation

The key to helping the hopeless is to embrace them with acceptance. Many years ago on my first evangelistic outreach with Youth With A Mission, I was part of a team of eight young people working for two weeks in the red-light district of Hamburg, Germany. Late one evening a friend and I left the coffeehouse we were based at and began to walk the streets, looking for someone to speak with or help. Our walk took us past a huge tavern full of boisterous sailors and prostitutes. As we hurried past this hub of raucous humanity we were startled to see a helpless-looking elderly woman standing next to the entryway of the tavern. My partner, fluent in German, suggested we offer to take the woman home or to a place of shelter. As we approached her, I estimated that she was about five feet tall. A stray lock of white hair protruded from under the dark scarf covering her head. She looked helpless and alone.

My friend asked her in German. "May we help you in some way? Are you lost, or do you need a taxi?"

The woman quickly looked up at us. I expected to see fear, or possibly incomprehension, on her face. Instead, the woman beamed a broad, grandmotherly smile at us and said, "Thanks for your offer, but no. I am fine. This is my home and mission field."

Immediately, my partner and I sensed we were in the presence of a saint. The woman's face was wide open, her eyes clear and full of love. She peered up at us, then asked, "Are you Christians?"

As we responded affirmatively, she reached out and pulled us toward her. "I thought so," she replied. "I can see the light of Jesus in your eyes."

"What do you mean, this is your mission field?" we asked her.

She then proceeded to tell us this story. "Many years ago when I was a young teenager, my parents were killed in the first great war. I had no remaining family, so I walked to a nearby convent and told the nuns I had no place to stay and no food to eat. They graciously invited me to move in with them. In fact, they helped me complete my schooling and then invited me to join the order. Their particular order had a ministry of helping the underprivileged. I loved my life there. It became my home. One day a few years ago, when I was seventy, the Lord spoke to me in the place of prayer. He said that I was to move on and begin my work as a missionary. I was shocked, assuming that I would live out my days in the convent. So I went to the mother superior and some other sisters to tell them what I had felt in prayer. They said they would pray with me for a number of weeks and ask God to confirm if this was from Him. Sure enough, after a couple of weeks we all felt God had spoken. I left the convent and followed God's leading to the city. The closest city was Hamburg. I asked God to show me the worst place in the city. That is how it came about that I am here."

As this woman of God continued to talk to us, I was struck by the combination of innocence, wisdom, and faith that she possessed. Her face radiated with joy. At one point a twinkle came into her eyes as she said, "You might not believe it, but I break up fights. A lot of times the sailors will get into a drunken brawl, usually over some woman. They often spill out onto the street, cursing and swinging their fists. I'm so tiny, I just burrow through the men until I find the ones fighting. I walk right in between them and push them apart. I say, 'Now boys. Let's calm down. There's nothing to get excited about.' And you know? It works every time!" At this, she broke into delighted laughter.

Then she became serious again. "My mission is to be the hands of Jesus, extended out to embrace the unloved and the unlovely. Often a drunk will be thrown from the tavern into the gutter. That's my signal to go into action. I wave down a taxi driver who helps me put the man into the taxi. We then drive two blocks up to my little apartment, take the drunken man upstairs, and let him sleep on a cot. When the man awakes from his stupor, I fix him coffee and soup. Then I tell him that Jesus loves and accepts him, even if nobody else does. And you know what? They always listen." Once again, she chuckled with genuine joy.

We spent about half an hour with this woman. I couldn't help but notice men and women passing us on the sidewalk. Many of them stopped and either bowed or nodded their head in reverence as they spotted their missionary friend. This woman had become a beacon of hope to many in this dark and ugly place. She didn't preach; she

> We are not forgiven... because we made ourselves forgivable or even because we had faith; we are forgiven solely because there is a Forgiver.
>
> —Robert Farrar Capon

loved. She didn't condemn; she accepted. She was a servant leader of wide influence in a place where no churches were to be found.

In the same way, Jesus was able to look through the outer shell of Zacchaeus' appearance and see the light of potential shining inside. As servant leaders, we too must choose to look beyond the fractured world of a person's current behavior and focus on the latent promise resident in all individuals. Initially, this requires accepting the *person* regardless of sinful behavior. The wonderful Catholic writer from the eighteenth century Francois de Fenelon says it so well:

> Charity does not demand of us that we should never see the faults of others; we must, in that case, put out our eyes. But it commands us to avoid attending unnecessarily to them, and that we be not blind to the good, while we are so clear-sighted to the evil that exists. We ought to remember what God can do from one moment to another for the most unworthy creature, and think how many causes we have to think ill of ourselves, and finally, we must consider that charity embraces the very lowest. It acknowledges that in the sight of God, the contempt that we indulge for others has in it something harsh and arrogant which extinguishes the spirit of Jesus Christ.[1]

Mere Tolerance or True Acceptance?

That which distinguishes biblically appropriate acceptance from unconcerned tolerance is compassion. Compassion, which literally means "to feel pain jointly," is the quality that allows one person to enter into the felt needs of another. It is a deep inner desire to identify with

---

1. Francois de Fenelon, *Fenelon's Spiritual Letters* (Christian Books Publishing House, 1982), p.229.

others in order to be a compassionate channel of healing to them. Biblical acceptance requires involvement.

Tolerance, on the other hand, is passive acquiescence, or a state of noninvolvement. It is an outward attempt to give credibility to a heart that is inwardly unconcerned. Jesus once said that many are called but few are chosen. I think it's also true that many are tolerated but few are accepted.

I once attended a luncheon meeting of ministry leaders and pastors in my city. A discussion ensued about the power of the gay community in city politics. As the discussion progressed, the language became militant and strident. One leader went so far as to declare that the gay agenda was to close all churches. At that point an eloquent African-American leader stood and spoke with great passion. "I've noticed that you who are attacking the gay community all come from suburban churches. All of my ministry is spent walking the streets of the inner city. I've not seen any of you on those streets. My staff and I spend part of our time helping in AIDS hospices. We bathe and change the bedding of gay men dying of AIDS. We speak of Jesus' love for them. I've not seen any of you there." He then sat down. The room became properly silent. The conviction of the Holy Spirit settled upon all of us.

Servant leaders cannot choose whether they will or will not become involved in the lives of people. Jesus, *the servant leader*, exemplified involvement in the act of incarnation. His act of "becoming nothing, taking the very nature of a servant"(Philippians 2:7)

> *Tolerance is the attitude of those who do not believe in anything.*
>
> —*G.K. Chesterton*

ensured his identity with us and involvement among us. Jesus entered into our very lives and felt our pain. He refused to distance himself.

With incisive insight, Henri Nouwen puts it this way: "The tragedy of Christian ministry is that many who are in great need, many who seek an attentive ear, a word of support, a forgiving embrace, a firm hand, a tender smile, or even a stuttering confession of inability to do more, often find their ministers distant men who do not want to burn their fingers."[2]

As leaders, are we conduits of the qualities that God has modeled for us through Jesus? Or are we unaware of and uninvolved in the lives of those we lead? Do our followers have to appease us to stay on our good side? Do we display disgust and disappointment when our followers do not perform to our expectations?

Acceptance, *involvement*, and *compassion* are three words that are indispensable in the vocabulary of the servant leader. But they are more than just words. They are attributes that flow daily from the servant leader's life to those he leads as he draws them on to new levels of spiritual growth and maturity.

2. Nouwen, *The Wounded Healer*, p. 71.

For Personal Study

1. Who in my life, by simply accepting me, helped me to grow as a person? For whom have I done the same?

2. Do I just tolerate people who irritate me, or do I make an active attempt to really understand them?

3. Have I ever been hurt by a leader who did not accept me? How did I respond to that leader? Have I hurt others by my refusal to accept them?

For Group Discussion

1. What are some differences between acceptance and tolerance? Share some situations in which you have seen the power of acceptance demonstrated.

2. Is there a difference between straightening people out and helping them grow? If so, what are some of the differences?

3. The need to belong is powerful in human beings. List some ways in which you could foster a sense of belonging in new people wishing to be a part of your church or ministry.

4. According to the quote from Francois de Fenelon, how should we handle the bad we see in other people? How does this relate to your personal experiences?

CHAPTER FOUR

The Perils of Favoritism

Angels can fly because they take themselves lightly.
—G.K. Chesterton

S alome placed the last of her dried fish in the basket along with the bread and the grapes, smiling with satisfaction as she did so. It would be enough food for the entire group. It was the last of her dried fish, and now that her sons were with Jesus most of the time, she wasn't sure when there would be more fish to replenish her stock. She didn't really mind. Her practical mind reasoned that short-term sacrifices were sometimes required to attain long-term security.

Everything was going according to plan. She pulled the door shut and made her way toward the northern quarter of the city. Her new white robe gleamed in the bright midday sun, and tendrils of black hair peeked from the edge of her scarf. She had taken extra care in grooming herself this morning.

Salome walked a mile before she spotted the group. They were just entering the house of Zadok. *Good,* she thought to herself. *They are retiring together for a rest. Jesus will be relaxed, and there will be no one else to distract him.* She quickened her pace and arrived at Zadok's door just as the servant was about to close it.

"My sons—I have come to see my sons," she said, glancing down at the basket. The elderly servant gave a toothless smile as he admitted her into the courtyard. Close to twenty men milled around in the coolness. She could see her sons talking energetically to a burly, rough-hewn fellow.

He must be the one they call "the Rock," she thought, recalling her sons' description of him. She moved closer. The Rock looked likable enough, but her sons had told her that Jesus found him impetuous and had to rebuke him on a number of occasions, sometimes in public.

A surge of satisfaction ran through her as she thought of Jesus rebuking this hulk of a man. It would never be necessary for him to rebuke her sons. She had raised them better than that. And if Jesus agreed, her efforts were going to be rewarded. Indeed, her sons were already well thought of by him. It was said that her elder son even held a special place in Jesus' heart.

As she approached, the Rock and her two sons turned to welcome her. The basket she was carrying made her doubly welcome. Her boys knew it undoubtedly held some of the delectable dried fish their mother was renowned for.

Salome greeted each of her sons. The two men couldn't help but notice their mother's preoccupation as she distractedly studied the courtyard beyond them. Her eyes darted back and forth, fixing the scene in her mind. It was as she imagined it would be. Some of the men were reclining, others were drawing water and drinking from two large earthen jars at the back of the courtyard. The atmosphere was relaxed and calm—perfect for carrying out their plan.

Salome motioned for her sons to come closer, and then she whispered, "Now's the right time. I will do the talking."

John looked a little uncomfortable. He would have preferred a more private place but knew better than to challenge his mother. And it had been his and James' idea in the first place, so they'd better be prepared to carry it through. They followed their mother as she made her way toward Jesus, who was alone, leaning against the wall at the side of the courtyard.

Salome had practiced this moment a thousand times in her mind. She knew what to do. Demurely, she approached Jesus, eyes lowered, arms extended, offering the basket of food.

"Master," she began in a clear and confident voice, "I have brought this food for the sustenance of you and your disciples."

Jesus focused his attention on her. "Thank you. The Father will reward you for this kindness."

Salome placed the basket at Jesus' feet and knelt down in front of him. Jesus picked up the basket and motioned for one of the disciples to come and take it. For a moment, John wanted to run. The plan they had devised seemed so tacky now.

Jesus returned his gaze to Salome. "What is it you want?" he asked in a soft and guileless tone. For a moment she felt reluctant to go on. Then the calming security of being flanked by her two sons restored her confidence. What she was about to ask for was, after all, on their behalf.

Salome stammered out the first few words as she collected herself, scrambling for the safety of her premeditated request. "Grant that one of these two sons of mine may sit at your right and another at your left in your kingdom." The anxiety of the moment had propelled the words from her mouth with a little more forcefulness than she had intended.

Jesus fastened his eyes firmly upon her, and the light of understanding shone brightly in them. He shifted his gaze to Salome's two sons standing on either side of their mother.

"You don't know what you are asking," he said to them. "Can you drink the cup I am going to drink?"

"Of course we can," the two brothers mumbled in unison, not exactly sure they understood the question but eager to meet the Master's prerequisites for power.

"You know that the Gentile rulers lord it over their people." Jesus' eyes stared directly, piercingly into the eyes of James and John.

"We already know that…" blurted James, a sense of frustration in his voice. Things were not going quite as planned.

"It is not that way among you." The Master's words sliced across their consciousness. "Whoever wants to become great among you must be your *servant*."

They were speechless, stunned at the choice of words used by Jesus. In confusion, they listened as he continued. "Just as the Son of Man did not come to be served but to serve."

In an instant John saw it clearly. Jesus was advocating a different way. This wasn't about having a position of prominence. It wasn't about thrones and titles. Jesus had never exercised his authority over them in the way of the elders or the Romans. What arrogance it was to presume that now he would begin to rank them over one another. Tears filled John's eyes as the revelation hit him.

"Forgive us," John spoke with quiet urgency as he helped his mother to her feet. The Master acknowledged John's contrition with a slight nod of approval. Then he wheeled away, leaving them to ponder his remarks.

The two men silently escorted their mother to the entrance of Zadok's house. Salome, as well, had some thinking to do. Weren't her sons collaborating with the man who would soon overthrow the Romans and restore peace and honor to Israel? She had willingly sacrificed her sons' livelihood to that end. Didn't Jesus owe them something in return?

Salome's shoulders were hunched as she, in confused disappointment, spoke her farewells. As James and John returned to the group, the Rock yelled to them: "Tell your mother she's welcome anytime. This fish is great!"

The temptation to gain special favor or to extend partial treatment can weave its seductive spell only upon the soul impressed with status.

Get Thee Behind Me, Status

Chapter two depicted the desire for status as a characteristic of wrong motives. The twin brother of status is favoritism. These two characteristics always accompany each other. We all know the verse that says, "God is no respecter of persons." Yet in the routine of daily events, leaders are often predisposed toward selective partiality in their relationships. Not only are we tempted to play favorites ourselves, but we also enjoy being the recipients of special favors granted by someone with status. Therefore, it is proper to ask these questions: Do people with perceived status receive special attention from me? Do I turn on the charm and offer kindness to those from whom I want or need something? Am I susceptible to being charmed into granting special favors?

James and John, along with their mother, were caught off guard by Jesus' response to the request for special treatment. Their mother's request was really, "When you assume the monarchy of the new Israeli kingdom, to what positions will you appoint my boys?" Jesus basically ignored the question, focusing instead on the theme of greatness as seen from God's perspective. His simple statement that service takes priority over position squelched all their fantasies of grandeur. Then, when he stated that even he, the son of God, did not come to be served but to serve, Jesus in effect declined to acknowledge his own status. How stark the difference between men's notions of kingdoms and God's call to *the* Kingdom!

Why Are These Leaders Acting So Strange?

I first became aware of the deception caused by status and partiality when I was nineteen years old. My parents took me with them to an annual denominational pastors' conference. I felt very comfortable at the first meeting. As I looked around, I knew most of the pastors present. Many of them had been guests in our home over the years.

After one of the evening sessions, we headed to a nearby restaurant for food and fellowship. As we sat together, my teenaged mind was confronted with a startling revelation. Pastors who had been so friendly when guests in our home now seemed barely civil. As I looked around, I quickly saw that the unfriendliest pastors were those with the biggest congregations. These pastors, along with several denominational officials, clustered together in cliques away from the others. The pastors of medium-sized churches also sat together. I could find no pastors of tiny churches or home mission works. They probably couldn't afford that restaurant. Incidentally, it also struck me that the leaders with the biggest name recognition were the noisiest group in the entire restaurant.[1]

Recently, my wife and I were invited to a wedding and reception. A number of so-called big-name people from

---

1. It would be an exaggeration to suggest that *all* pastors of large churches act this way. It just happend to be that way on this occasion.

the church world were in attendance. In what looked like a Theater of the Absurd, adults jockeyed for positions of proximity to the celebrities. Smiles grew brighter and laughter more pronounced as people basked in the glow of a famous person. I have watched the same phenomenon occur at major Christian conventions, where status was conferred in proportion to the size of entourage following in the wake of God's-Special-Vessel-at-This-Particular-Moment.

Status is such a blind spot for the evangelical church today. I used to think that this was a uniquely Western failure. Now, after years of travel on five continents, I see it's the same everywhere. It takes a conscious effort to resist the compelling magnetism of the status and power that come through position.

No Task Too Small

Lisa is a vibrant and talented woman who serves with Youth With A Mission. She recently shared with me about her early days in the mission. Her primary work duty was in the housekeeping department at one of our large ministry centers overseas. During those early days, she felt lonely and isolated. Another American woman, the wife of one of the leaders, supervised that department. Lisa tried to reach out to her for friendship and support. Alas, this other woman seemed to have time for nothing but the most cursory of remarks.

Ten years later, Lisa and the leader's wife met at a large international conference. By that time, Lisa had found her niche and had become well known. During one of the sessions at the conference, Lisa was introduced to the gathered crowd. The leader's wife came to her afterward, laughed nervously, and said, "You know, you look so familiar. I can't quite place you. You look like someone I had cleaning for me at one of our centers, but that's ridiculous." She laughed again.

Lisa looked into the eyes of the person she had once wanted as a friend and replied, "No, it's not ridiculous. That's exactly where we met. You were supervisor of the housekeeping department." The other woman became flustered and soon excused herself from the conversation.

What is so ridiculous about the idea that a person could be cleaning toilets one day and have an "important ministry" the next—or vice versa? Preparation for ruling and reigning with Christ does not begin with ruling and reigning. It begins *and ends* with service. Even the rightful Ruler of the universe, Jesus himself, does not divorce his service from his rulership. His nonstop place of service as our intercessor should be proof enough. If, in the course of our service, God should place us in a position of leadership, how can we consider any task as too menial?

Richard Foster states it well: "The ministry of small things must be prior to and more valued than the ministry of power. Without this perspective we will view power as a 'big deal.' Make no mistake, the religion of the 'big deal' stands in opposition to the way of Christ."[2] The leader who wants to do only big things for God reveals the true nature of his motives. He also falls prey to a shallow narrowness of thinking. "There is no real elevation of mind in a contempt of little things; it is, on the contrary, from too narrow views that we consider those things of little importance, which have in fact such extensive consequences."[3]

The true servant leader views no person as incidental, nor does he believe in chance meetings. Each engagement

---

2. Richard J. Foster, *Money, Sex, and Power* (San Francisco: Harper and Row Publishers, 1985), p. 219.

3. Fenelon, *Fenelon's Spiritual Letters*, p. 204.

with another person is seen as an opportunity to express Christlikeness with no preference given because of status, position, race, gender, or denominational affiliation. Leaders beguiled by position soon expose their motives by their partiality and favoritism. James, however, tells us succinctly: "My brothers, as believers in our glorious Lord Jesus Christ, don't show favoritism" (James 2:1). Further on in the same chapter he makes the point that partiality is a violation of the royal law of love (James 2:8–9). He then sums things up by listing the traits of heavenly wisdom in James 3:17: "But the wisdom from heaven is first of all pure; then peace loving, considerate, submissive, full of mercy and good fruit, *impartial* and sincere."

Servanthood is the antidote to the disease of status seeking that infects elements of the body of Christ. The servant leader is one who follows in the footsteps of Jesus, not the steps that lead to the top of the corporate ladder. Again, the words of Richard Foster are so appropriate: "Servant leaders are people who are servants before they are leaders and will be servants when the tenure of leadership is concluded."[4]

> *He let himself get distracted by any "nobody" he came across, whether a hemorrhaging woman who shyly touched his robe or a blind beggar who made a nuisance of himself.*
>
> —*Philip Yancey*

---

4. Foster, *Money, Sex, and Power*, p. 243.

For Personal Study

1. Do I confer favoritism on people within my sphere of influence? How does this affect those outside the circle of favoritism?

2. Have I ever tried to gain special favor from someone I viewed as having something I needed? Did that situation build or destroy the relationship?

3. Have I been guilty of manipulation by attempting to "butter up" someone in a position of influence? Is this a tendency of mine that needs changing?

For Group Discussion

1. Discuss the religion of the "big deal" to which Richard Foster referred. What does this mean, and how does it damage the cause of Christ?

2. What is the difference between being appropriately serious about our ministry and taking ourselves too seriously? In what ways can taking ourselves too seriously hinder our motive for serving?

3. There is a clear link between favoritism and racism. Discuss why this is so, and give examples of the damage this does to both society and the Church.

CHAPTER FIVE

On the Receiving End

The supernatural virtue of justice consists of behaving exactly as though there were equality when one is stronger in an unequal relationship.
—*Simone Weil*

Simon of Bethany greeted Jesus at the entrance to his palatial home. The rings on his fingers glittered in the midday sun. Simon's greeting was purposely reserved as he motioned Jesus inside.

The host kept his eyes diverted from the large brass basin at the door. Normally he called his servant to wash the feet of his guests, and he had debated whether he should do it for Jesus. Finally, he had decided against it. He wasn't sure that it was proper for him, a Pharisee, to honor this particular guest in that way. He didn't want to give Jesus the wrong idea.

Simon had also given thought to what his friends would think. Jesus came from a mediocre heritage with family still in Nazareth. Although Simon was curious to learn more about Jesus, he wanted to do so on his own terms. He did not want it thought that he was giving Jesus any form of endorsement.

Still, as he walked past the empty basin, he could not help but feel uncomfortable. Thankfully, his guest did not appear to notice anything out of the ordinary, and soon they were seated together at the table.

Simon surveyed the meal with a sense of satisfaction. Each dish, meticulously prepared, spoke of his status. It pleased him greatly, and he wondered whether the Teacher realized how lucky he was to be a guest in this home.

An awkward silence fell between the two men as they began eating. Simon began to wonder why he had invited Jesus at all, since Jesus seemed almost oblivious to the honor of being in the home of one of the wealthiest and most influential men in town. Simon wasn't even sure anymore what he had wanted to ask the Teacher.

Simon's thoughts were interrupted by the sound of scuffling feet behind him. Simon assumed it to be an overzealous servant bringing the next course before they had finished eating the current one. Without turning to acknowledge the servant, Simon raised his hand as a signal to stop. Perplexed when the noise of the scuffling footsteps did not recede, he turned, only to see a woman who had no place in his home.

Disgust registered on Simon's face. He had seen the woman many times waiting outside the west gate, vying for customers. Now, this whore was in his house. How did she get in? What did she want?

Before Simon could decide how to deal with the situation, the woman had stopped in front of Jesus. She knelt at his feet and drew an alabaster flask from beneath her tunic. She then placed the flask beside Jesus' feet and looked up into the Teacher's eyes. The apprehension etched upon her once beautiful face was met with compassion on his. The woman buried her head in her hands and cried uncontrollably.

Simon beckoned for a servant. This was outrageous! It was meant to be a private dinner, and now a prostitute was turning it into a fiasco. Simon beckoned again, his irritation deepening. He glanced at his guest. How embarrassed the Teacher must feel. But when Simon looked closely at Jesus, he found he could not interpret the expression he saw.

The prostitute loosened the stopper on the flask and began pouring the contents over the Teacher's feet. Tears and oil mingled as she massaged Jesus' feet. At a different time and place, her actions would have appeared sensuous. But this time, they seemed more like an act of worship.

The woman reached up and unfastened her hair clasp. Her long, black hair tumbled free. She lowered her head and began wiping the oil and tears from Jesus' feet with her hair.

Now Simon was furious! First, this woman had the audacity to enter his home uninvited. Second, the Teacher must be a fraud. He, Simon, had been fooled into entertaining a fraud! A man with any spiritual discernment, and certainly one who paraded around as the Son of God, would know that it was a prostitute groveling at his feet.

Simon was still scowling when Jesus turned to him. "Do you see this woman? I came into your house. You did not give me any water for my feet, but she wet my feet with her tears and wiped them with her hair. You did not give me a kiss of greeting, but this woman, from the time she entered, has not stopped kissing my feet. You did not put oil on my head, but she has poured precious perfume on my feet. Therefore, I tell you, her many sins have been forgiven—for she loved much."

Simon seethed with anger and embarrassment. His guest was clearly inferring that this woman had shown more hospitality than he. It was an outrage, an insult! Simon was in his own home, and the Teacher was making him feel like a sinner.

The leader willing to receive ministry from a follower—be it encouragement, correction, or instruction—elevates the follower to a place of worth and usefulness in God's kingdom. Simultaneously he removes himself from the pedestal of inflated self-importance.

The High and Mighty Syndrome

Have you ever been around a leader who projects the imperial air of a Very Important Person? By mannerisms and body language, such an individual casts a calculated aura of untouchable spiritual magnitude. He *wants* others to know how special he is. While the person may use the language of servanthood, he always places himself in a position where only he can dispense ministry. Therefore, both his words and his actions are condescending. If such a person does receive ministry from others, it will be only from those of similar rank and privilege, certainly not from those "below" him!

Simon (and the Pharisees) would have fit this mold. Despite the fact that Simon had invited Jesus into his house as a guest, he wouldn't allow himself to get too close. He was unsure of Jesus' real stature as a leader and certainly wasn't going to open up and receive from him until he was sure that Jesus was at least an equal.

However, as we see in the vignette, Jesus refused to be impressed by this type of gamesmanship. He allowed a well-known prostitute to minister to him. It is typical to think of Jesus as doing all the ministering. We forget that he also often received ministry from others. Luke tells us: "The twelve were with him, and also some women who had been cured of evil spirits and diseases: Mary (called Magdalene) from whom seven demons had come out; Joanna the wife of Cuza, the manager of Herod's household; Susanna, and many others. These women were helping to support them out of their own means" (Luke 8:1–3).

Unfortunately, it is the tendency of many spiritual leaders today to view only one side of the coin with regard to ministry. Jesus taught that it is better to give than to receive. But our egotistical interpretation of this in relation to leadership and ministry often blinds us to the fact that we need the humility to graciously receive ministry from others—even from those whom we feel have not achieved our level of maturity. The carnal leader detests the appearance of being either in a subordinate position or in a place of need when surrounded by subordinates. (Please note: The word *subordinate* has no place in the language of the Kingdom. I use it here merely to emphasize that leaders need to be secure enough to switch roles with those they view as "under" them.)

A servant leader, on the other hand, understands that he, in common with all humanity, always stands in the place of need. In addition, he recognizes that humbly receiving ministry from a follower actually allows the follower to grow in confidence. In other words, we humbly receive from a "subordinate" for his sake as well as for our own sake. Thus, unconcerned with image, the servant leader

> *Nothing is ever influenced in just one direction.*
>
> —*Peter Senge*

unflinchingly acknowledges his own need and is not afraid to place himself in a subordinate role if it will help someone else grow into wholeness.

The Lonely Leader

Frank was a self-sufficient person, a pastor with a happy family and a growing ministry. As far as I could tell from the outside, everything was falling into place for him. Yet one day Frank asked me to come to his house to talk. As I sat across from Frank in his study I could tell that something was troubling him.

We chatted for a few minutes until Frank finally took a deep breath and said, "I don't think I can take it anymore. I don't know why I ever got into the ministry in the first place." He stopped to gauge my reaction, which I tried not to show.

"The other day I was given a couple of tickets to a ball game," he continued, "and I wanted to take a buddy with me. Do you know, I couldn't think of anyone to take! Sure, there are a lot of people who do what I tell them, but I don't have a single close friend—someone I can talk to, someone I can share my problems with." I nodded sympathetically, having felt the same way myself at times.

Frank continued, "It never used to be this way. In college and when I was first married, I had lots of friends. But since I became a pastor, nobody wants to spend time with me anymore."

As the conversation progressed, we pinpointed the source of Frank's loneliness. He had fallen into the trap so many other Christian leaders have fallen into. He had put himself "above" his congregation and no longer felt he was able to be himself around them. He now had an image to protect. What would the congregation do if they knew he lost his temper at his teenage son or if they knew he was not as regular as he should be in prayer and Bible study? Frank believed his congregation would not look up to him if he failed to project an image of perfect leadership.

The exact opposite is true. Nobody wants to spend time with a person who is projecting an image rather than being real. Most of us would rather have a leader who is flawed but real than one who appears flawless but is phony. God is the only perfect leader, the only one with the strength of character to handle perfection. The human leader who endeavors to project an image of perfection places himself under an enormous burden that will eventually break him.

My wonderful father was a pastor for fifty years. Several years before he died he had an opportunity to hear me teach on servant leadership. At the conclusion of the service Dad wanted to talk. "You know," he started, "in all of my years in the ministry I had never before heard a sermon on servant leadership. In fact, everything I was taught in Bible college about leadership is opposite to what you teach. I was told that to be a good pastor, you had to keep a distance between yourself and your congregation. So that's what I did. I was always available to pray for or counsel people, but I never really got close to them. I regret that now."

In my biased estimation, my father was a very solid and effective pastor. Yet he hit upon a key point that is still being propagated in some Bible colleges and seminaries today. The thinking goes like this: If, as a leader, you get too close to your followers, they will not respect you as much. Therefore, they will no longer follow you. I have two simple questions to ask: How involved was Jesus in the lives of his disciples? And did he keep his distance in an endeavor to make people respect him?

Even Jesus had times of admitted weakness. Consider the time when he was about to be crucified. He prayed, "If it is possible, may this cup be taken from me." In today's language, Jesus may well have said something like this: "I really don't want to go to the cross. I'm scared and alone. Isn't there any other way?" By these honest words, Jesus was displaying vulnerability, not failure. Further, he asked several of the disciples to accompany him. Jesus was not afraid to let his followers see him at his worst. In fact, this was part of the discipling process.

Accountability Is a Two-Way Street

Today, we often see the opposite. As Gayle Erwin puts it: "In our society (church and secular), the higher you go up the ladder, the more inaccessible you are to people—the more hidden your personal life is."[1] Ironically, some of the most inaccessible leaders are the ones who demand the greatest accountability from those "under" them. Accountability is a watchword for such leaders. They demand accountability from those under them but are deliberately inaccessible to those same people. Thus, accountability goes only one direction—upward.

One-way accountability is the single most dangerous element found in many leadership structures of today. Let me propose several reasons why this is true. First, it is dangerous to the leader himself because it places him in a Godlike role that only God is able to fill righteously. Over a period of time, the leader in this type of system will usually develop a secret life that is at odds with his message to others. When this happens, the poison of self-deception begins its inexorable takeover.

Second, one-way accountability invariably leads to authoritarian abuses of power. This happens with even the best-intentioned person because of the corrupting influence that unilateral power develops in the heart of fallen mankind. Because the leader is not practicing what he

---

1. Gayle D. Erwin, *The Jesus Style* (Word Books, 1983), p. 73.

preaches ("You must be accountable"), he lives by an automatic double standard. Some leaders attempt to get around this by establishing a long-distance link with a spiritual leader who becomes their mentor. (I am aware of one system in which a person refers to the spiritual leader to whom he is accountable as his "father.") When challenged on this issue, such a leader will say, "I, too, am a man under authority." The problem, of course, with long-distance leadership is that *it doesn't work* over a long period of time. This is especially true if the mentor receives communication *only* from the leader under his charge.

Let's say Pastor Smith has a congregation in Oregon but considers himself to be under the leadership of Bishop Jones in Texas. The bishop calls the pastor once a month to get a report. If Pastor Smith is guilty of authoritarian abuses of power, do you think he is going to tell that to the bishop, especially if he is trying to impress him? Perhaps, the pastor is not even aware that his leadership style has evolved toward authoritarianism. The only people who can really hold the pastor accountable are those who know the truth of what is transpiring on a daily basis. Wouldn't that be the people *in the pastor's congregation*? And would it not also include the pastor's own immediate staff?

The servant leader is willing to expose his humanity, including his fears and failings. He realizes that his followers are ultimately to look not to him as their leader but to the one true leader—Christ. Therefore, the need to look impressive is *not* a part of the thinking of a servant leader.

What About the "S" Word?

Countless horror stories now abound in the Body of Christ of people who have been bludgeoned by the word *submit*. The principle of submission has been turned into a cardinal doctrine of many churches and ministries. The irony is that many who teach a convoluted doctrine of submission are often the very ones who attack the concept of papal infallibility that they believe Roman Catholics practice. The only difference is that they go *far beyond* anything the Roman Catholic Church teaches on this subject. Pope John Paul would never be so arrogant as to tell people whether or not they can buy a new house or whom they should marry or when they can take a vacation. Yet I know of numerous evangelical ministries that have actually gone this far in the name of submission.

In the New Testament, the principle of submission does *not* have to do primarily with obedience and control. The Greek word used most often for submission is *hupotasso*. Two English words that help qualify this particular type of submission are *voluntary* and *mutual*. Paul uses this word in Ephesians 5:21: "*Submit* to one another out of reverence for Christ." Notice the aspect of mutuality. The person who walks in submission of this type communicates an attitude of humility and collaboration in interchange with others. Paul uses the exact same word in the next verse when he says to wives, "Wives, *submit* to your husbands as to the Lord." The nuances of this word in the Greek language were startling to the people steeped in the Jewish culture of that day. The concept of a *voluntary yielding for the sake of love* was practically unheard of at that time, especially between husband and wife. Up to this point, the culture dictated that the wife had no choice but to come under the domination and control of the husband. Paul was actually liberating wives by telling them of a new kind of relationship based not on mere duty but upon the mutual and voluntary choice to love.

The people of that era were also familiar with a different word that is translated as *submit*. The word is *hupotage*, which has to do with control and obedience. Paul used this word in Galatians 2:5 when he said, "We did not give in [submit or obey] to them for a moment." He was speaking of the strong pressure on the part of the Judaizers who were compelling Gentiles to become Jewish before converting to Christianity. This particular word for submit is *never* applied in the New Testament to the relationship of leader/follower. In fact, it's not even used to describe the relationship of man to God![2]

Yet, today many leaders teach that you must "come under" your leader in obedience to him. Some leaders call this the *"principle of covering"* which is meant to convey the idea that a divine protection or umbrella of authority comes over those who walk in obedience to their leader. Further, this teaching states that when you are under your covering (meaning a leader, usually male) you are not really responsible for your choices because your leader takes that responsibility. This concept, which has the weight of a doctrine in some circles, is almost non-existent in the writings of orthodox Christianity before the 1960s. The "proofs" for this teaching come from a suspicious mixture of unrelated incidents in Scripture: the historical account of a pillar of fire and a cloud leading the Israelites through the wilderness; David's telling his men

---

2. *Hupotasso* is used 38 times in the New American Standard Bible. In addition to Eph. 5:21 and 24, examples of it may be seen in Titus 3:1, 1 Peter 5:5, and Romans 13:1. Each usage is voluntary, not necessarily obligatory, meaning that failure to not submit in this way is not a sin. *Hupotage*, which contains the ideas of control and obedience, is used only four times—Galatians 2:5, 1 Timothy 2:11, 3:4, and 2 Corinthians 9:13. An idea which relates conceptually to the words for submission is the Greek word *peitho*. This word is translated obey or obeying four times. Twenty-nine times it is translated, have confidence in or be persuaded by. Hebrews 13:17 says, "Obey your leaders and submit to their authority." The word *obey* is *peitho*. The word *submit* used here is the Greek *hupeiko*. This is its only place of usage and it means to yield, retire, or withdraw.

not to kill God's anointed leader, King Saul; Jesus' description of himself as the good shepherd; and Paul's admonition to the church at Corinth that women wear a covering over their heads. Put these accounts together and you have the modern-day concept that followers are to come under the control/covering of human leaders!

In contrast, listen again to the words of Gayle Erwin: "When Jesus alludes to submission, it is always directed toward leaders or the ones who want to be great in the kingdom, and they are always ordered to submit downward, not upward."[3] Is this not the attitude of Jesus that Paul says in Philippians 2:5–7 we are all to have? "Your attitude should be the same as that of Christ Jesus: Who, being in very nature God, did not consider equality with God something to be grasped, but made himself nothing, taking the very nature of a servant." This kind of submission has its origins in heaven. In the Godhead, mutual submission is the norm, not the exception, because it is an act of love. When a person is taught to come under the dominion of another human being, let's call it what it is— cultish control. This is *not* a New Testament principle.

A proper submission does exist where the servant leader practices rather than preaches. It is a submission rooted in humility and has to do with being a learner. The servant leader knows that he always has much to learn. He is never an expert but instead wants to grow in understanding. Therefore, he will endeavor to learn from anyone he meets. In that sense, he submits to all in his desire to acquire greater understanding. This does not mean that he obeys all. The

> *Dictators ride to and from upon tigers which they dare not dismount. And the tigers are getting hungry.*
>
> —*Winston Churchill*

3. Erwin, *The Jesus Style*, p. 55.

word *disciple* comes from a Greek word that means learner.[4] The true disciple is one who has the humility to learn from others.

---

4. The Greek word for disciple is *mathetes*. It comes from another Greek word *manthano*, meaning to learn, to find out.

For Personal Study

1. Have I given some people in my life who really know me permission to speak clearly to me about my failings?

2. What fruit has appropriate teaching on submission borne in my life? If I have been hurt by an extreme form of submission teaching, am I now free from the effects of that teaching?

3. Do I consistently allow people to minister to me even if they are relatively young Christians? Can I receive their ministry without reminding them that I have been a Christian longer than they have?

4. Is there a relationship gap between me and those I lead? If so, what has contributed to that gap?

5. When in a follower role, do I contribute to the growth of my leader? In what ways?

For Group Discussion

1. How is accountability lived out in your current context? Should you be less or more accountable?

2. Describe for the rest of the group a time when you observed a leader receive ministry from someone "under" that leader's ministry. How did you feel at the time? Was the leader truly vulnerable, or was he only trying to appear humble?

3. What results of authoritarian abuses of power have you witnessed?

4. In your current ministry or leadership, are there checks and balances in place around those in top leadership? If you are the top leader in a situation, how does this apply to you?

5. Meditate upon the description of Jesus' attitude in Philippians 2:5-8, then share your understanding of what it means to have the nature and attitude of a servant.

CHAPTER SIX

No Compromise

Gold defiles with frequent touch;
There's nothing fouls the hand so much.
—Jonathan Swift

A cold winter wind hurled tiny grains of sand against the huddled figures on the narrow road leading from the village. The travelers winced as the full force of the blustering wind belted them. Jesus and the disciples were retreating from a village that was still buzzing with animated fervor at what it had seen and heard.

In the midst of the excitement, Jesus had slipped quietly away. Judas was accustomed to it by now. He used to get extremely angry when Jesus retreated from ministry activity, but now, like the others, he had learned to accept it.

As the group struggled on, Judas was oblivious to the gathering wind. His mind was caught up with the fact that he and his companions had left town so hurriedly that they hadn't had time to buy food for the journey. And even if they had, there wasn't enough money in the purse to pay for it.

The situation greatly frustrated Judas. Things seemed so disorganized around Jesus. Here they were, heading off into the countryside with no food or money. If they had stayed a little longer in the village, they would surely have been invited to eat at someone's home. But it was always like this. Jesus seemed unaware of their real needs. Sometimes Judas felt like shaking him and telling him to wake up. Instead, he just followed along, a sea of frustration tinged with bitterness building inside him.

The group did not realize it, but as they receded into the swirling dust, someone was watching them. The observer's face would have stood out in any crowd—handsome and bearing the unmistakable lines of wealth, self-confidence, and aristocracy. The luxurious cape and opulently bejeweled fingers couldn't conceal the confusion that lingered in the man's eyes as he watched Jesus depart.

"Sir, sir!" he yelled after the group in a vain hope to be heard. He was used to people scurrying to obey his every word. But the Rabbi kept walking, and the wind threw the man's words back in his face. The man began running after Jesus, his body straining against the steady headwind.

"Sir!" he called again as he got closer. At last Jesus heard him. He turned and waited for the young man to catch up. Jesus recognized him as the rich young man who had been lingering at the edge of the crowd in the village.

Stumbling awkwardly, the young man fell onto his knees before Jesus. "Good teacher," he panted, "what must I do to inherit eternal life?"

Judas and Peter exchanged glances. Why couldn't this man have asked his question earlier in the village instead of waiting until they were on the road in the midst of a gathering storm? Once again Judas felt exasperation. If they had stayed in the village a little longer, this rich young man would surely have invited them to dine with him.

Jesus placed his hands on the man's shoulders and looked deeply into his eyes. "Why do you call me good? No one is good—except God alone." The young man nodded, lowering his gaze to the ground. He knew the implications of the Master's statement.

"You know the commandments: 'Do not commit adultery, do not murder, do not steal, do not give false testimony, honor your father and mother,'" Jesus continued.

"All these I have kept since I was a boy," the young man replied, a hint of frustration in his voice. He had always followed the priest's requirements, but still, something was missing—something vital. He had hoped Jesus could point out what it was.

Suddenly the potential of the situation dawned upon Judas and brought a smile to his face. This was better than anything he could have planned. Here was what appeared to be an extraordinarily rich young man sniveling at Jesus' feet, begging for instruction on how to receive eternal life. All the Master needed to do was say the word and Judas was sure the man would collect his belongings and join the group. Their penny-pinching days would be over. This man would be able to furnish the money to meet the group's needs, and they would never lack for anything again. This was their God-given opportunity. Judas only hoped Jesus had the common sense to see it for what it was and offer the invitation. Sometimes, though, Jesus was so naive, so witless about these things that Judas decided he had better seize the moment.

"Teacher," Judas said as he stepped in beside Jesus. "Could I talk to you now? Alone? It's a matter of some urgency."

Jesus turned and looked at Judas. It was a look that would have turned away a less-determined person. "It will only take a moment," Judas persisted.

With a sigh, Jesus turned back to the rich young man. "You still lack one thing." At last, here was the missing link in his quest for righteousness. "Sell everything you have…" Judas whispered a silent prayer of relief and thanks. "…and give it to the poor, and you will have treasure in heaven. *Then* come follow me."

At that moment, bewilderment and anguish registered simultaneously—on two faces!

⸎

The servant leader will resist the temptation to gain personal financial advancement from ministry opportunities, knowing that to compromise integrity is to lose the ministry.

Oh, Be Careful Little Hands What You Seize!

The servant leader is obligated by a motive of purity to detach his personal financial comfort from all ministry situations. Jesus' refusal to take advantage of an impressionable, rich young ruler serves as a stunning reminder that purity and integrity in financial matters will forbid us from manipulating the message of the Kingdom for personal gain. Sadly, the prevalence of fiscal impropriety—subtle in development but devastating in effect—has been the devil's weapon of choice in ambushing countless leaders. Far too many leaders find out too late that the soil of financial compromise is filled with quicksand.

The degree of trust conferred upon a leader by a follower often provides situations that the unscrupulous leader can easily exploit to private advantage. Once a leader surrenders to this temptation and begins to justify self-serving actions, a deadly new factor will be released upon him—the dominating spirit of mammon. Richard Foster says it this way:

> When the Bible refers to money as a power, it does not mean something vague or impersonal. Nor does it mean power in the sense we mean when we speak, for example, of "purchasing power." No, according to Jesus and all the writers of the New Testament, behind money are very real spiritual forces that energize it and give it a life of its own. Hence, money is an active agent; it is a law unto itself; and it is capable of inspiring devotion.[1]

The power of mammon was much in evidence at a Christian social function I attended a few years ago. In the crowd were a number of wealthy Christian philanthropists. It was painfully embarrassing to watch several ministry leaders who needed money to support their ministries approach the wealthy. Smiles broadened, eyes sparkled with flirtatious affability, and there was an obvious tendency to laugh too quickly in false exuberance. It is one thing to directly and humbly request financial aid; it is quite another to manipulatively use "ministry" or flattery as a means to financial gain.

The apostle Paul was very aware of the potential to muddy the waters between ministry and financial gain. J. Oswald Sanders makes the following observation of Paul:

> Paul was very conscious of the ubiquitous problem, and was therefore scrupulous in his financial dealings and his stewardship. In order to remove from the young churches the burden of his

---

1. Foster, *Money, Sex, and Power*, p. 26.

support, he earned his own living, and at times he supported his colleagues as well. He was "financially clean," setting a noble example of generosity.[2]

Salesman or Servant?

Far too many of today's spiritual leaders go astray at this point. After decades of being exposed to the consumer mentality that defines contemporary America, some Christians adapt their theology to accommodate accumulation. One current notion is that material blessing is a sign of spiritual strength. A leader friend told me of a church from which he received a $25,000 honorarium for giving a forty-minute sermon. Further, he stated that in that particular circle of churches, the pastors gave each other these amounts to prove to each other that their respective congregations were in the flow of God's blessing. Is this true generosity, or is it opulence? Philanthropy, or ostentation?

The same attitude has been elevated to an art form in some media-driven ministries. The lower-middle-class Christian-television viewer tunes in faithfully to hear her favorite preacher.[3] When it is time for the financial appeal, the camera zooms in close, showing the sincerity and gravity of the preacher's face. An emotionally charged story is usually told, followed by a declaration that God is obligated to bless viewers who send money immediately. Thus, the wonderful concept of generosity is twisted into a caricature

> *Most people would succeed in small things if they were not troubled by great ambition.*
>
> *—Henry Wadsworth Longfellow*

---

2. J. Oswald Sanders, *Paul the Leader* (NavPress, 1984), p. 140.
3. The average viewer of religious television is profiled as a 55-65 year old widow or divorcee living just below the federal poverty line.

wherein Christian leaders are seen as con artists, and their followers as deluded people wanting to be duped.

The Bible contains no recorded instance of Jesus directing his followers to give material things, not even food or money, to him. Jesus' motivation was love and compassion toward others, not personal acquisition. Nor did Jesus request money for the perpetuation of his ministry. Can you imagine Jesus looking with all seriousness into a television camera and stating, "If you don't give to this ministry, we'll have to shut down, and millions of souls will go into a Godless eternity"?

"No one can serve two masters. Either he will hate the one and love the other, or he will be devoted to the one and despise the other. You cannot serve both God and Money" (Matthew 6:24). This was Jesus' summation of the matter. If we are to be servant leaders of Christ, we must deal ruthlessly with the motivations of our heart, especially in the area of our attachment to mammon. To fail to do so is to stray from the path so clearly laid out by our Lord. Recent events of financial betrayal in the Body of Christ clearly show the results of devastation and ruin for the materialistic leader and his followers.

For Personal Study

1. Have I used my position to gain financial advantage?

2. Do I receive special benefits as a leader that others in my ministry do not receive? If others in my ministry knew about these benefits, how would they feel?

3. How do those who know me the most view my integrity? How do creditors?

For Group Discussion

1. How open should a church or ministry be about its finances? How detailed should those receiving donations be in reporting to their donors?

2. What kind of limitations should be applied to legitimate requests for financial assistance?

3. How would you define mammon from scripture? Is mammon money, or is it a spiritual force that attaches to money? Is it greed?

CHAPTER SEVEN

Let Your Actions Do the Talking

When being is divorced from doing, pious thoughts become an adequate substitute for washing dirty feet.
—*Brennan Manning*

P eter entered the room, breathless and late. He had gone to the market to buy bread for supper, and it had taken him longer than expected.

The room was as he had hoped. Sarah, the wife of a wealthy trader, had offered her home for the occasion. The dwelling was not opulent but was richly furnished with many foreign items that Sarah's husband had brought home from his various trips. Peter smiled to himself. This was more like it. At last, things were beginning to come together for the group.

Peter had started out with such high hopes. The Master had healed people, cast out demons, and talked of a new Kingdom that was coming. But over the past six months, it seemed that events were less exciting. A subtle change had come over Jesus. There was more talk about counting the cost and serving others, but not nearly the number of miracles as at first. Peter found it a little disturbing but assumed that it was part of the training process. Maybe the Master was testing their loyalty, making sure they were ready. They needed to pass through this phase before the "good things" began—and they had begun!

Nothing else in Peter's life compared to the feeling of strutting beside Jesus as the group entered Jerusalem. Peter relived the experience repeatedly in his mind: The frenzy of the people clamoring to lay down their robes in front of Jesus. The children ripping branches from nearby palm trees to wave exuberantly at them. And the way the crowd shouted, "Hosanna! Blessed is he who comes in the name of the Lord, even the King of Israel." Yes, Peter reminded himself, they were shouting *King*. Finally the Master's obscurity was over, His reign about to begin.

Peter surveyed the room. These were the twelve men the Master was going to take with him to the top, and Peter, a fisherman, was one of them. Those who served others were now about to be served. It was perfect, better than Peter could have wished had he planned it himself.

Peter placed the bread next to the other food on the table and sat down beside James. "There's plenty more where that came from," he said, sinking into the luxurious red cushion. "As soon as the baker realized I was with the Master, he wouldn't hear of taking payment for the bread. He even said we could come back anytime for more and he wouldn't charge us. That's the way it will be from now on. Everyone wants to be in the Master's favor. They're calling him the next King of Israel, you know?" Peter smiled broadly. Ah, yes, things were looking up!

Peter ate heartily as the conversation continued around him. Some were talking about the authoritative way that Jesus had overturned the trading tables in the court of the Gentiles. Others were making plans for the future now that the tide had turned for them.

Unnoticed in the midst of the hubbub, the Master rose and made his way out of the room. He reappeared several minutes later, his chest bare and a towel wrapped around his waist. Walking deliberately over to the corner, he poured fresh water into a clay basin. As Jesus picked up the basin, an abrupt silence fell upon the group.

Peter wondered what the Master was doing now. Jesus looked for all the world like a common servant. He knelt in front of Judas and motioned for him to place his foot in the basin. Judas looked terribly uncomfortable as the Master began to wash his feet. As the Master continued, Judas' discomfort turned into agitation.

All eyes in the room were fixed on Jesus. What was this all about? The men watched Jesus pour a dipper of water over Judas' feet and then tenderly wipe them dry with the towel he had wrapped around his waist. The Master carried the basin to the next person, John. As he bent down to wash John's feet, he spoke lovingly. "You do not realize now what I am doing, but later you will understand."

Peter was repelled by the scene. This was their Master, the one they were calling the new King of Israel, and he was on his knees washing their feet as if he were the lowliest servant in the household! There was no way he, Peter, would lower himself to do the job of a common servant.

Peter was next in line, and he could see it coming. But Peter wanted none of it. Embarrassment aside, it just wasn't right! No man—least of all a man with the importance of the Master—should have to wash his followers' feet. That's what servants were for.

The Master dried John's feet and pushed the basin toward Peter. "No," Peter said firmly, looking straight into the Master's eyes. "You will never wash my feet."

Jesus looked up at Peter's face. Gently and patiently he said, "Unless I wash you, you have no part with me."

The room was quiet. Outside, the laughter of children could be heard. Peter sat stiffly. He knew he must be missing something. Then, slowly at first, past conversations came to Peter's mind. *The last shall be first. Except you become as a child. He who would be great among you must be your servant.* Illumination began to flood Peter. This wasn't really about washing dirty feet. It was about humility, about taking the lesser path, even when glory was in sight. Now he understood what the Master was doing! "Peter, if I do not wash your feet, you can have no part with me," the Master repeated.

Peter's reply was barely audible to the others: "Then, Lord, not just my feet but my hands and my head as well."

As Peter spoke, the resistance seemed to seep out of him. Peter sat quietly and allowed Jesus to minister to him while the other disciples watched in studied silence.

Finally, the Master was done. He rose to his feet, rubbing his back. Then he spoke to all the disciples: "Do you understand what I have done for you? You call me 'Teacher' and 'Lord,' and rightly so, for that is what I am. Now that I, your Lord and Teacher, have washed your feet, you also should wash one another's feet. I have set you an example that you should do as I have done for you."

When words predominate, actions are slighted. When actions predominate, words bear witness.

Your Actions Speak So Loud, I Can't Hear What You're Saying

The concept of superstar that dominates the current view of leadership has done a grave disservice to the New

Testament ideal of leadership. Coupled with the outrageous excesses of much teaching on submission to authority, many church settings have produced leaders who are untouchable and followers who are passive spectators. The gap of understanding between pulpit and pew has widened to such a degree that leadership is seen as a lofty fantasy accessible only to those rare individuals having supernatural reserves of charisma and communication skill.

However, merely being able to engagingly transfer information is only part of the picture in terms of Christian leadership. Communication, as shown by Jesus, is about the *impartation of ourselves*. Because of this, training others for leadership cannot be linked only to the structure of a Sunday morning church service.

The proper—and most effective—setting for teaching others about Christian leadership is found in simple, everyday activities by which the practical and relevant nature of a relationship with God can be modeled. The servant leader must think, eat, breathe, and sleep *modeling*, for it is the medium for training future leaders.

In the New Testament context, leadership implies discipleship, and discipleship as modeled by Jesus applies to *all* areas of a person's life. It is impossible, therefore, for a leader to disciple someone else when he is seen only in a "hero" role. As stated earlier, leadership viewed primarily as a position is usually seen as a position "at the top," held for one hour one day a week. But what about the other twenty-three hours of a leader's day? What about the other six days of the leader's week? Leadership training requires that a leader be seen in pain as well as in victory, in crisis as well as in calm, and in sorrow as well as in joy. In other words, leadership training encompasses all of life.

The servant leader places utmost priority in being a living demonstration of the relationship between verbal instruction and day-to-day life. Because role modeling is minimized in the classroom but maximized in everyday life, the servant leader will always be looking for ways to use the situation at hand to exemplify biblical truth.

Numerous sociological studies confirm that human beings learn most readily by observing role models. In the way children need interactive guidance from their parents, followers need guidance and role modeling from their leaders. A setting wherein the follower sees the leader only at the front of a group "leading" both distorts and negates the effectiveness of leadership dynamics. Unfortunately, too many leaders are in the habit of using the sermon or lecture as the primary format for instructing those in their charge.

The perfect leader, Jesus, lived and responded to all of life's challenges in complete openness before the disciples. His responses to people were no different on the street than they were in the synagogue. The disciples observed the same consistent Jesus, whether at a party or in prayer.

Six Principles for Effective Modeling

One of the best books I know of on church leadership was written by Lawrence Richards.[1] In his book, Dr. Richards outlines six principles for effective modeling. As I read his theories about how effective modeling takes place, I marveled at how completely Jesus modeled the life of faith

> *Talkers are not good doers.*
>
> —*Shakespeare*

for his followers. When Christ stood after washing the disciples' feet, he had truly earned the right to say, "I have set you an example that you should do as I have done for

---

1. Dr. Lawrence Richards, *Church Leadership: Following the Example of Jesus Christ* (Zondervan, 1988).

you." Prayerfully examine these six principles set forth by Lawrence Richards, using them as a guide to see whether you are an effective model for those whom you would train.

1. Frequent, long-term contact with the model.

As Jesus began his three years of public ministry, he gathered disciples around him. Many of these followers were with Jesus only part of the time, on occasion returning to their fishing or other means of livelihood. Jesus named twelve as his "inner circle," but as we read through Scripture, we find examples of many other people following Jesus. The twelve, along with others like Joseph of Arimathea, Martha, and Mary, enjoyed frequent, consistent contact with Jesus.

2. A warm, loving relationship with the model.

Jesus often challenged the disciples about their motives, often reproved their impulsiveness, and at times ignored their questions. Yet there is no doubt that he deeply loved those whom he trained, even when they were unlovable. He washed the feet of a doubter, a traitor, and a loudmouth, and by his service, he won their hearts.

3. Exposure to the inner states of the model.

It is easy to copy outward techniques of leadership. But Jesus knew that leadership was more than an outward appearance. Throughout the gospels, we see that Jesus was approachable and allowed people to see him for who he was. The gospel writers describe for us times when Jesus was depressed, tired, angry, and weary, as well as loving and caring. In short, they saw him as a normal person responding to the various situations of life that he encountered. Jesus wasn't ashamed to have people observe his responses.

4. Observation of the model in a variety of settings.

"The Word became flesh and lived for a while among us...full of grace and truth" (John 1:14). Jesus found himself in just about every conceivable situation. He mixed freely with prostitutes, Pharisees, Samaritans, rulers, fishermen, farmers, housewives, tax collectors, and thieves. His disciples were with him in a storm, in the field, and at the synagogue. Jesus was a model in everyday situations, and his message was always rooted in the circumstance at hand. Money, travel, hospitality, crisis, pain: Jesus used each of these to give living demonstrations of how a leader should respond.

5. Consistency in the model's behavior.

The principle of consistency requires that external situations not alter relationships. Jesus was consistent in his obedience to the will of the Father, even when it meant going to the cross. His own pain did not prevent him from observing the plight of others and then loving them in their plight.

6. A correlation between the standards of the model and the standards of the group.

Jesus did not preach one message to his followers while secretly living another. Rather, he lived like they did. When he told them to take no money with them, neither did he. When he commanded them to heal the sick, he had already done the same. There is no instance of Jesus setting a standard for his followers that was greater than he himself lived. Jesus lived a lifestyle commensurate with his proclamation.

Humility in the Model

Because we are human beings living on a fallen planet, there will be times when our actions are not consistent with our words. That is where the fruit of humility must come into play. A current definition for humility states that humility is the willingness to be known for who we really are. Which is better: to hide behind a facade of perfect spirituality or to allow people to really know us as we are, problems and all?

On the surface, the typical person reasons like this: "I have a lot of personal problems. If people know what I'm really like, they will withdraw from me. Therefore, I will not allow people to get too close." The paradox of humility, like servant leadership, is that the closer people get, the more they will trust us. Trust always comes with knowledge. The more we know someone, the more we understand. With understanding, trust develops.

Accountability is another invaluable advantage of servant leadership. I make myself accountable by inviting others to scrutinize my life. If there are areas where I need improvement, those who know me best can speak most clearly to my problems. As applied to the concept of modeling, a leader who is unteachable cannot sustain a modeling relationship for long. A follower will tolerate genuine flaws in a leader but will eventually withdraw from the phony facade of a leader unwilling to receive correction.

Unfortunately, much of the emphasis on accountability today is in the context of structures and flowcharts. For a servant leader, however, accountability has more to do with relationships than with structures.

> *Humility is the most difficult of all virtues to achieve; nothing dies harder than the desire to think well of oneself.*
>
> —*T.S. Eliot*

Effective role modeling presupposes a close relationship between leader and follower and therefore serves as a protection to both. If we truly desire to have an impact on the lives of others, we must be prepared to spread our life before them. Jesus "dwelled among them as one who serves."

For Personal Study

1. Am I a better talker than a doer? In what areas do my actions not back up what I teach or preach?

2. Do those I lead see me in a variety of everyday settings, or do they see me only when I am in an up-front leadership role?

3. Other than my parents, who have been my most influential models? What did they model, both positive and negative?

4. When my behavior is not consistent with what I teach, do I cover up the truth or do I let my followers know that I have feet of clay?

5. For parents: Would my children say that I am the same at home as I am in ministry activities?

For Group Study

1. Is there such a thing as someone who is called only to preach?

2. What are some characteristics of humility, and how can they be exhibited by leaders?

3. What are you looking for in a role model?

4. Why are people generally more upset with a leader who makes mistakes and then covers them up than they are with a leader who makes mistakes and admits them?

CHAPTER EIGHT

The Meekness Factor

Heroing is one of the shortest-lived professions there is.
—Will Rogers

Peter stirred in his sleep. He had been vaguely aware as he lay down that something was not right. Now, in the early hours of the morning, he scoured his mind for what it could be. What was it that had been troubling him? His fuzzy mind couldn't seem to recall. A voice cut through his searching thoughts. "Are you still sleeping?"

Peter groggily opened his eyes to see the Master staring down at him. Suddenly, everything came rushing back. Jesus had asked them to stay and pray with him, but one by one they had succumbed to fatigue. Guilt flooded Peter.

The Master had been very agitated last night. Peter had never seen him that way. Jesus had talked almost incoherently about betrayal and death. Peter knew he should have made the effort to stay awake with the Master, but he had been unable to keep his eyes open any longer.

It was obvious the Master had not slept. Even in the moonlight Peter could see his bloodshot eyes and his shoulders sagging with exhaustion.

Jesus' voice was filled with resignation. "The hour has come. The Son of Man is betrayed into the hands of sinners. Rise! Let us go! Here comes my betrayer!" He gestured to his left.

Peter turned and saw a group of people coming over the brow of the hill, their burning torches marking their progress. Peter hurriedly roused the other disciples from their slumber. As the crowd approached, Peter hoisted a sword from his belt and took his place beside Jesus. He recognized several he knew among the crowd. Some of the chief priest's servants, a number of soldiers, and other well-known rabble-rousers from Jerusalem were carrying torches, lanterns, clubs and other weapons.

Peter winced when he saw the size of the mob. His little band was outnumbered by at least five to one. Was this why the Master had been so melancholy? Was this the end? Was it all over for them?

Judas stepped from the midst of the approaching crowd and walked up to Jesus, his eyes darting nervously from side to side. He came close enough for Peter to hear his out-of-breath salutation. "Greetings, Rabbi!" Judas said shakily as he embraced and kissed the Master.

With a wistful smile upon his face, Jesus replied, "Friend, do what you came to do." Judas evaded the Master's gaze as he took a step backward. Aza, the high priest's servant, moved forward to orchestrate the arrest. Pandemonium broke out. Men yelled and ran toward the Master, their clubs held high. Two of the largest men, special guards from the temple, attacked Jesus.

Overcome by anger, Peter quickly assessed the situation, looking for a way to escape. Once he could free the

Master, they could make a run for it. Tightening his grip, Peter swung his sword at one of the guards. The razor-edged sword crashed against the guard's skull, sending the man to his knees. Blood spurted from the guard's head, and his ear fell into the dust at his feet. Glad for the distraction, Peter tugged at the Master. "It's now or never. Let's get out of here."

But Jesus did not move. He stood before them, the hem of his robe splattered with blood and his eyes fixed on the high priest's servant. Aza felt uneasy and strangely out of control, though he was supposed to be in charge.

The Master approached the injured guard. The group fell silent, sensing that something significant was about to happen. The Master picked up the mutilated ear, wiped it on his robe, and reached out to the suffering soldier. Jesus gently placed the man's ear in the correct position and pressed it with his palm. The bleeding immediately stopped. Jesus held his hand over the ear a few seconds, and when he drew his hand back, the crowd gasped. The guard's ear was completely healed. There were no marks, no scars, nothing to indicate that only moments ago it had been sliced off with a sword.

Aza coughed nervously. He had a job to do, and a little trickery was not going to deter him. But neither of the guards heeded him when he motioned for them to arrest the Master.

"Put your sword back in its place," said the Master, turning to Peter. Then, looking directly at Aza, he said: "For all who draw the sword will die by the sword. Don't you think that I could appeal to my Father, and he would send more than twelve legions of angels to rescue me? But then how would Scripture be fulfilled?"

Aza fumed. "Seize him," he barked to the guards. The guards shook their heads and retreated into the crowd.

They no longer had the stomach for this. Other guards stepped forward to take their place, and Jesus was led away. Peter and the other disciples followed, baffled by the night's events.

⤜⤛⤜

The leader who walks in meekness is forever liberated from the need to use his position as a platform from which he can get back at those who have hurt him or taken advantage of him.

The Facts Are Not Always the Truth

If you had been in the Garden of Gethsemane that night, how would you have interpreted Jesus' actions? If Jesus truly had enough power to reattach a soldier's ear, surely he had enough power to save himself from the situation. But why didn't he use that power? He had the resources to alter the outcome but made a deliberate choice not to use them. Many would view this as weakness. The Bible describes it as meekness.

"Have you ever noticed the number of times Jesus refused to use power?" asks Richard Foster. A few paragraphs later he goes on to say: "The power that comes from above is not filled with bravado and bombast. It lacks the symbols of human authority; indeed, its symbols are a manger and a cross. It is power that is not recognized as power. It is a self-chosen position of meekness that to human eyes looks powerless. The power from above leads from weakness."[1]

I remember vividly my first encounter with meekness. I was eight years old and lived in a neighborhood bursting

---

1. Foster, *Money, Sex, and Power,* p. 203-204.

with boys my own age. All of us were sports fanatics who spent every spare moment honing our imagined athletic skills on the crudely assembled basketball court at Eric's house. Eric was my hero. At seventeen, he was the only big guy in the neighborhood.

One sunny Saturday we all gathered at the court for a game. Eric was there, accompanied by his brother-in-law. Because Eric and his brother-in-law were the tallest, they were on opposite sides, guarding each other.

The game was close and competitive. In fact, it began to get rough. At one point, Eric and his brother-in-law were battling for a rebound when suddenly the brother-in-law exploded with anger. He turned on Eric and began pummeling him in the face. We little guys were stunned. It wasn't just the anger of the brother-in-law that shocked us. It was also Eric's response: he put his hands down at his sides and passively allowed the punches to bloody his face.

Finally, I couldn't stand it a moment longer. I yelled, "Come on, Eric. Fight back. You're tougher than he is. What's the matter? Are you a chicken?"

Eric stoically stood his ground until his brother-in-law jumped into his car and raced off. The gang of eight-year-olds silently disappeared, stunned at the swiftness of Eric's defeat.

I followed Eric inside his house. Eric walked calmly over to the sink and turned on the faucet. He winced as he began to wash the blood from his face.

"Why didn't you fight back?" I asked, completely baffled by Eric's nonresistance.

Eric turned to look at me through swollen, purple eyes. "I'll tell you why," he said. "A couple of months ago we got into a fight over something he said about my sister. I did pretty well. But when it was over, he told me that if I ever stood up to him again, he would go home and beat up my sister. I knew he meant it. I really love my sister and don't ever want to see her hurt. Therefore, I decided that I'm not ever going to be the cause of my sister getting beat up."

My young mind reeled with newfound insight. Eric really was a hero. His apparent weakness in receiving the beating was not the true picture. Mere facts do not always adequately explain the truth. The *fact* was that Eric did get beat up. The *truth* was that Eric could have retaliated, but he exercised strength of character to restrain himself to protect someone he loved. Eric was meek but not weak. A lesser person might have buckled during the beating and begun swinging his fists, but not Eric. Compassion for his sister restrained him.

The same was true of Jesus at the time of his arrest. Legions of angels could have come to his rescue had he just given the word. I imagine the disciples could have put up a good fight in their own right, but self-control restrained Jesus. Since something higher was at stake, Jesus willingly submitted to his arrest.

Servant leaders must take their lead from the Master's example. True meekness is one characteristic of the servant leader. But what does it mean to lead from the place of meekness? It obviously does not mean that a leader should be a spineless individual with weak resolve. Nor does it mean that he should be indecisive and hesitant while mumbling pious platitudes about being a servant.

Scottish preacher James S. Stewart sums it up this way: "It is always upon human weakness and humiliation, not human strength and confidence, that God chooses to build his kingdom; and that he can use us not merely in spite of our ordinariness and helplessness and disqualifying infirmities, but precisely because of them."[2]

---

2. Sanders, *Paul the Leader*, p. 173-174.

Because of this principle, true biblical leadership often goes unnoticed or misinterpreted. The reason is simple: fallen man is a hero worshiper and, as such, is drawn to heroic, larger-than-life images. Knowing this, Satan attempted to lure Jesus away from the quiet path of the cross and onto the world stage of fanfare. The tantalizing temptations served up by the enemy were all centered in spectacular feats designed to induce hero worship. Had Jesus succumbed to the allure of showy displays of omnipotent power, the world would have indeed followed him—right to the pinnacle of megalomania! It is no wonder, then, that those in attendance at the crucifixion were an unsympathetic mob, most anxious to hurl cruel insults at Jesus. From their limited perspective, Jesus was weak—an object of scorn rather than honor.

The Humility/Meekness Link

In Scripture, humility and meekness are closely related. Both have to do with submission. Humility is concerned primarily with the vertical relationship of man to God. As stated in 1 Peter 5:6, "Humble yourselves, therefore, under God's mighty hand." Leadership, and all other acts of service in God's Kingdom, is measured by humility.

Meekness, on the other hand, is a fruit of God's grace that is exhibited primarily in the horizontal relationship of man to man. Charles Finney wrote: Meekness, a phenomenon of the will, and as an attribute of

> After crosses and losses, men become humbler and wiser.
>
> —Benjamin Franklin

benevolence, is the opposite both of resistance to injury and retaliation. It is properly and strictly forbearance under injurious treatment.[3]

---

3. Charles G. Finney, *Lectures on Systematic Theology* (Colporter Kemp, 1944), p. 169.

Injurious treatment always comes from other human beings. At times, someone may attempt to take advantage of someone else by revealing the person's weaknesses to others. The meek person does not fear the truth, even about himself. While he may feel a sense of betrayal at being exposed by someone he allowed to view him in a vulnerable state, his meekness forbids him from retaliating.

"But," someone may ask, "if a leader allows his followers to see him in a vulnerable state, won't the followers use that against the leader at a later time?" The answer is simple—"Yes, the risk is great!" The fine line between humility and humiliation resides in the choice one makes to be either open or closed in regard to personal realities. Those who initiate self-disclosure acquire the fruit of humility. Those who protect themselves often become humiliated.

Jesus knew the risk yet made himself vulnerable, even to Judas. Further, despite knowing that within twenty-four hours Peter, James, and John would all deny knowing him, Jesus allowed them to see his anguish at Gethsemane. How amazing that after the Resurrection, Jesus did not remind the disciples of their failure. "I told you so" was not part of Jesus' vocabulary.

Beyond the truth of the humility/meekness principle lies another equally important truth: God deliberately chooses the weak to fulfill his purposes. According to Paul in 1 Corinthians 1:26–29:

> Brothers, think of what you were when you were called. Not many of you were wise by human standards; not many were influential; not many were of noble birth. But God chose the foolish things of the world to shame the wise; God chose the weak things of the world to shame the strong. He chose the lowly things of this world and the

despised things—and the things that are not—to nullify the things that are, so that no one may boast before him.

J. Oswald Sanders reinforces this truth by stating, "Although Paul himself was an intellectual, he gloried in the fact that God had purposefully not chosen the intellectual, highborn, powerful, and influential. Instead he chose people who were weak in ability, influence, or even in body—those disregarded by the world—to achieve his purposes of blessing."[4]

For the servant leader, leading from meekness means that the leader is totally honest with himself and others about his own weakness, seeking neither to cover it up nor to flaunt it in a self-pitying way. He moves ahead in loving obedience to God in spite of his frailty, therefore of necessity abandoning himself to God's power and grace. Lasting fruit is never harvested consistently by self-reliant planters, but only by those who understand that God's "power is made perfect in weakness" (2 Corinthians 12:9).

Servant leadership does not require that we cease using our natural, God-given gifts. It does require that we cease our *reliance* upon them. Humility and meekness are the qualities that put us in the place of proper dependency upon God. They are also the qualities that will eventually qualify us to rule and reign with Christ. Jesus told us in the Beatitudes that the "meek will inherit the earth." What is the reason behind this, another

> *The doorstep to the temple of wisdom is a knowledge of our own ignorance.*
>
> —*Charles Spurgeon*

paradox? I believe that the meek will be the only people with the strength of character to rule without their egos getting in the way.

---

4. Sanders, *Paul the Leader*, p. 175.

Perhaps another example from J. Oswald Sanders will illustrate:

> Dwight L. Moody, the Billy Graham of his day, learned to exploit the power of weakness as Paul did. He was innocent of education, his physical appearance was unattractive, and his voice was high-pitched and nasal. But his conscious weakness did not prevent God from shaking the world through him.
>
> On one occasion, a press reporter was assigned to cover his campaigns in order to discover the secret of his extraordinary power and influence over people of all social strata. After he returned from his assignment, he wrote, "I can see nothing whatever in Moody to account for his marvelous work."
>
> When Moody was told this, he chuckled, "Of course not, because the work was God's, not mine." Moody's weakness was God's weapon.[5]

---

5. Sanders, *Paul the Leader*, p. 176.

For Personal Study

1. Have I exhibited meekness in relationships with those in my ministry, especially those who have caused me discomfort, or have I used retaliation as a way to put the troublemakers in their place?

2. Deep inside, have I secretly wanted my followers to view me as a hero? In what ways have I promoted a hero image about myself?

3. Has my ministry and leadership relied primarily upon natural ability, or are there elements of my ministry for which God is the only explanation?

4. Have I ever flaunted my ministry strengths or leadership position in order to impress someone else?

For Group Discussion

1. Discuss why meekness and humility serve as checks and balances to a person serving in a leadership position. Why is this necessary?

2. In what ways should a leader respond when hurt or criticized by those working with him?

3. How should a leader balance being vulnerable with having necessary boundaries? Should a leader always be accessible to everyone? If not, what are some qualifying factors?

4. Why is it true, as Spurgeon said, that "the doorstep to the temple of wisdom is a knowledge of our own ignorance?"

5. Look at the context (2 Cor. 12:1-10) of Paul's statement that "...power is made perfect in weakness." What specific issues was Paul addressing? How should we as modern-day leaders deal with any "thorn in the flesh" we possess?

CHAPTER NINE

Having Faith Enough to Trust

*We are raised, reconciled, and restored not because we are thrifty, brave, clean, and reverent but because we are dead and our life is hid with Christ in God— because, that is, Jesus has this absolute **thing** about raising the dead.*
—Robert Farrar Capon

The three men sat huddled together in the corner on the floor. Golden slivers of sunlight burst through the cracks in the shutters, casting pools of light onto the dusty floor. It was dawn, but the men had been awake for hours, just sitting and staring into the darkness.

"Who would have thought it would end like this?" Bartholomew said, voicing his thoughts aloud. "A week ago we were part of the huge welcome—the palm leaves, the cheering, and the accolades."

"Do not be afraid, O Daughter of Zion; see, your king is coming, seated on a donkey's colt," intoned Philip, more for his own hearing than anyone else's.

Bartholomew slammed the side of his fist against the

floor. "Why didn't we see it? We could have stopped Judas had we known."

Philip shrugged his shoulders. "There was no way of knowing. Did you see the way the guards greeted him? They acted like old friends."

"Joseph told me the chief priest gave Judas thirty pieces of silver for his effort." Tears flooded Bartholomew's eyes as he spoke.

"Well, Judas got what he deserved. I hear they found him hanging from a tree. Killed himself," offered Philip, hoping the news would in some way atone for the treachery of their former comrade.

"We should all be dead," interjected Peter, speaking for the first time. "I was just as bad. When the Master asked me to pray with him in the garden, I fell asleep. We all did. If we had stayed awake, things might have been different. We couldn't even stay awake when he wanted us to." Peter shook his head in remorse, then paused to collect his thoughts.

"And then when I was sitting in the courtyard and the servant girl asked me if I was with him, I said no. What was the point of aligning myself with a doomed man? I did it twice more after that. But you know what the worst part was? Jesus knew. He *knew*. He knew I would do that." Peter glanced at his two colleagues, dark, shadowy lumps in the gloomy room. "The night he washed our feet, he knew. He told me then that I would betray him three times. And he knew what Judas was up to. It was as if he wanted it to happen. I don't understand how, but he knew. He saw we'd each betray him in our own way."

The room became silent. The disciples' comfort with one another now played against them. Each knew what the others were thinking and what they had done. There was no hiding behind a curtain of lies, no need for pretense.

What was there to live for now? They had all left their livelihoods to follow Jesus. They had believed he was the Messiah and that they were part of a vast new order he would bring to change the world. Now it was over, and they were all partly to blame.

"I wish I could go back. I should have stayed with him at the cross," said Bartholomew after a few minutes. "I didn't even have the courage to do that. His mother stayed with him, but I didn't…"

"We are marked men, whether we were with him at the end or not," interjected Peter. "Yesterday the guards came to my uncle's house asking for me. He told them he hadn't seen me for days, but they searched anyway, turning the place upside down."

"Do you think it's safer for us to stick together or to go our separate ways?" asked Philip. Somehow they needed to pull their thoughts together. The three men were in great danger.

The city swarmed with soldiers and indignant Jewish leaders. Priests and Roman soldiers made an absurd but deadly alliance. And now that they had blood on their hands, they were likely to want the problem dealt with completely. They wouldn't want the "Christ problem" to raise its head again, and the remaining disciples might attempt to keep the controversy alive.

"I don't know about the Master. I don't think anything we could have done would have saved him," said Bartholomew, ignoring Philip's question. "I watched him. It was as if he wanted to die in the end. When Pilate was asking him questions, he wouldn't answer. Pilate pressed him hard. I think he wanted to let the Master go, but the Master would say nothing."

The men slumped into silence once more. Their emotions swirled from grief over the betrayal of their Master to contempt and anger for the one who had betrayed him. But more than anything else, they felt an intolerable burden—*each* had betrayed the Master. Cowardice, unreliability, feebleness, and fear were no longer abstract concepts reserved for others who were weaker. The pain they were all experiencing denied them the luxury of pointing the finger at anyone else. When the harsh, unrelenting beam of adversity glared upon the men, all their character flaws were mercilessly exposed.

The disciples talked for hours, lapsing in and out of grief, anger, frustration, and disappointment. Finally, they agreed that it would be less dangerous if they stayed together as a group. Alone, they could be picked off. As a group, they could defend one another.

It took more than a day before word reached all the scattered disciples. Chaos reigned in Jerusalem. The rumor mill was spinning. There were all kinds of conflicting reports. Some said Jesus' body had been stolen by his disciples. Others said he had risen and his graveclothes were wadded up in the tomb. Whatever the explanation, one thing became clear on the third day: the tomb where they had buried the Master was now empty. Peter went to see for himself. There was no logical explanation. Peter walked away, scratching his head and pondering.

Finally, the disciples made their way to the prearranged meeting place. When the last one arrived, James heaved the door shut and dropped a heavy wooden bar into place. If anyone wanted to enter now, they would have to contend with a four-inch-thick door.

James turned and surveyed his comrades. It was the first time they had been together since the night of betrayal. How different they all looked now. John's haggard face showed deep anguish. Thomas wore a poker face, trying his best to appear composed. Who would be the first to speak? Peter? James looked around, spotting his burly friend. "*He doesn't look that bad*," thought James to himself. In fact, he appeared animated, even cheerful. James raised his eyebrows; there was no telling what grief and guilt could do to a person.

Peter cleared his throat and abruptly stood to his feet. A broad smile creased his face as he began. "Like you, at first my heart was torn. Now I understand." The other disciples listened, unsure of the direction Peter was taking them. "Yesterday I was on my way to Emmaus with another man who had once been a follower of the Master. I was confused by all that had happened and wanted to leave it behind."

Philip and Bartholomew looked at each other. Peter was the one who had finally insisted that they all stay together in Jerusalem.

"As we walked along, we were joined by a man who didn't seem to know anything about what had gone on with the Master. So we began filling him in." Peter could not contain the excitement he felt. His gestures emphasized the importance of his words.

"Finally we came to an inn and stopped for something to eat. As we sat with the stranger to eat, he took bread, gave thanks for it, and offered each of us a piece. At that moment, I realized I had seen this happen once before. A cloud seemed to lift from over us. The stranger was the Master! But before I could say anything, he disappeared."

"Are you sure?" asked Andrew.

"I won't believe it until I see him with my own eyes," grumbled Thomas. "And why didn't you recognize him right away?"

"Let Peter talk. I want to hear," interjected James. "This fits with the things Mary Magdalene said."

Peter opened his mouth. But before he could speak, another voice sounded in the room: "Peace be with you!"

The disciples stared at the One who spoke, their eyes wide, their mouths agape. It was the Master!

Jesus held his hands out to them. Each disciple recognized those hands. They were hands that had reached out lovingly and tenderly to them many times before. Now, a jagged scar marred their symmetry. No, not marred... *adorned*.

A collective gasp escaped from the lips of the stunned disciples, followed immediately by the dawning of joyous revelation. The men's eyes were still wide but no longer fearful. An intoxicating wave of joy rolled over them.

Peter watched as the Master surveyed the room. Jesus' eyes rested fondly upon each disciple. When his gaze reached Peter, the Master stopped and looked penetratingly at him. Peter could feel the tears welling in his eyes. He looked back at Jesus, a question forming in his mind. *Me, Lord? After all I have done? Me? You still want me to follow you?*

There was no need for Peter to voice the question; the Master had read it in his eyes. Jesus nodded gently, and Peter felt the glow of God's trust and acceptance wash over him. A flood of tears cascaded down his cheeks, and the burly fisherman unashamedly fell at the feet of his Master.

*T*rust conferred is an act of emancipation;
trust betrayed, an act of violence.

Lord of the Second Chance

Jesus placed the responsibility for establishing his Church in the unsure hands of eleven abject failures. David Watson aptly describes the situation:

The disciples of Jesus were very ordinary people, with all the human faults and failings that we often see in ourselves. Because of the integrity of the Gospels, we see the disciples as ambitious, selfish, argumentative, weak in faith, anxious, fearful, impulsive, immature in words and actions, proud in the face of temptation, lethargic in prayer, impatient with the children, weary of crowds, bewildered and depressed by the events leading to the crucifixion. We notice how slow they were to learn, how quickly they forgot even the most dramatic spiritual lessons. In other words, they were just like most of us! Yet these were the men that Jesus chose to to be disciples and trained to be leaders.[1]

It is truly remarkable that God chose to use the eleven disciples to change the world forever. It is even more astonishing that he chooses to use us! In one of his letters to the Corinthians, Paul voices amazement that God would use sinful men. "For God, who said, 'Let light shine out of darkness,' made his light shine in our hearts to give us the light of the knowledge of the glory of God in the face of Christ. But we have this treasure in jars of clay to show that this all-surpassing power is from God and not from us" (2 Corinthians 4:6–7).

Jesus' leadership example, as shown through the way he entrusted his perfect message to imperfect men, may be the hardest principle of all for us to emulate. Jesus modeled, trained, commissioned—then he *left*! The apostle Paul later copied this technique. In fact, most of Paul's leadership was exercised from jail cells! What a contrast to the methods we employ today.

1. David Watson, *Called and Committed: World-Changing Discipleship* (Wheaton: Harold Shaw Publishers, 1982), p. 49.

Although we are all imperfect, our tendency is to demand perfection from others before trusting and releasing them into leadership. It will be a long wait if perfectionism taints our training! Our current practice is to train, train, and train some more. After training, some leaders keep holding on to their trainees by telling them they owe allegiance to those who trained them. In other words, we want those we train to be attached to our ministry—at least until they begin to be a problem to us.

What is the fruit of our leadership in terms of training and releasing? Do we take joy in seeing our followers embark upon their own ministries even if they never relate to us as their leader again? Are we thrilled or threatened when they eclipse our leadership in terms of scope and influence? If we release our trainees into leadership responsibility and they perform imperfectly, do we recall them or disown them?

The Experience Barrier

A common criticism that arises during discussions about releasing people—especially young people—into leadership roles is that they don't have enough experience to lead. Let me ask an obvious question: How will they ever acquire experience in leading if they are not allowed to experience leading? Could it be that some leaders are afraid to give others, especially youth, a chance to lead for fear that they might err and in erring be an embarrassment to the one who released them? Isn't such a fear rooted in a self-centered desire to protect one's own reputation rather than in a desire to guard against releasing a leader prematurely?

Like Jesus, the servant leader will always resist the inclination to load increasingly stringent qualifications on potential leaders. He wants to free his trainees, not bind them with weights too heavy to bear. He understands that a major part of leadership is to provide an atmosphere of trust and freedom. Only in such an environment can leadership develop to its full potential.

Too often, leaders do the opposite. They erect an extensive framework of qualifications, ostensibly to better prepare the prospective young leader for his job. If the young leader survives such rigorous training, it is to his credit, not to the training itself. The sad irony is that if the older leader had faced similar demands when he was young, he probably could not have fulfilled them.[2]

In God We Trust—How About People?

Trust is the most fragile component in the mix of ingredients that make up healthy relationships.[3] If reciprocal trust is absent, insecurity will set the mood of a relationship. The servant leader understands that honor and trust always go together. Therefore, the servant leader seeks to honor his followers by both investing trust in them and demonstrating his own trustworthiness. This trust is best demonstrated by training a follower and then releasing him into increasing levels of leadership. Leaders sometimes get mixed up at this point. They often attempt to teach trust by *demanding* that the follower trust the leader unquestioningly. The problem with this is that trust demanded but not extended leaves the follower with a sense of violation.

This brings us to an important principle. *The initial responsibility of demonstrating trust must first rest with the individual possessing the greatest authority.*[4] A leader confers

---

2. Take the time to study Matthew 23 and see what Jesus had to say about this type of leadership. The strongest language Jesus ever used was employed in addressing leaders who weigh people down with religious conformity.

3. From lectures given by Tom Marshall in Amsterdam, Holland, May 1987.

4. Ibid.

honor upon his followers when he proves his own trust-worthiness to them. However, when a leader betrays trust, his followers are shamed and dishonored.

Several years ago two well-known television evange-lists were exposed for wrongdoing. One of those leaders stood before his congregation after getting caught and confessed his sin. This leader's denomination was pre-pared to take this man through a rehabilitation program on the condition that he step down from leadership for a period of time. I recall watching a prominent Christian television host attack the leader's denomination, stating that it did not need to start a rehabilitation process. The man's reasoning was that because God forgave the leader, the denomination should, too. Therefore, the leader should be back in the pulpit immediately. I couldn't help disagreeing. The issue here is not forgiveness but trust. When trust is violated, especially by a leader, the ensuing damage cannot be stopped by forgiveness alone. Trust has to be repaired over a period of time. A major rupture of relationship takes place whenever trust is violated. This becomes an issue of betrayal.

On the other hand, when a leader extends trust, the relationship of follower to leader deepens. The follower will usually endeavor to live up to the trust extended to him and will begin to identify at a deeper level with the leader.

You're the Leader

During my first outreach with Youth With A Mission, I was a participant in such a situation. Though quite immature, I was assigned to be the leader of a team of young people going into Paris, France to do street evange-lism. The only housing available for the two-week outreach was an old, dilapidated theater that had been converted into a church. The facilities were woefully inadequate, having only one restroom with a cold-water sink and a toilet.

Three days into the outreach, Loren Cunningham (founder of Youth With A Mission) arrived to visit our team. I was excited to see him and even more excited to learn that he was planning to spend a few days. I didn't yet know Loren well, and I expected him to stay in a hotel. It came as quite a shock when he asked me, "Denny, where do you want me to sleep?"

"What do you mean, where do I want you to sleep?" I stammered, embarrassed to have to explain our inadequate facilities. "You're the boss of Youth With A Mission. Don't you sleep wherever you want?"

I will never forget the patient, gentle look on Loren's face as he replied, "No, Denny. You're the leader of this team. While I am here, I am under your leadership. Where do you want me to sleep?"

I was stunned, but there was no place of honor that I could allocate to Loren as his quarters. "Follow me," I finally instructed him, as I headed up some dingy stairs. The women on the team had placed their sleeping bags in the balcony and walled off that area with sheets. We single men had set up our quarters on the stage at the front of the theater in an attempt to separate from the women. The platform area was rather small, and each of us had defined our personal "space" by an assortment of carefully placed suitcases, sleeping bags, and chairs.

I was about to offer my carefully defended spot to Loren when I noticed him eyeing the grand piano. Surely he didn't want us to move it! There was nowhere for it to go. Instead, Loren bent down and examined the space available *under* the piano. Without thinking, I blurted out, "You can put your sleeping bag under the piano, if you like." Loren nodded, smiled graciously, and said, "That sounds just fine to me."

Even though that incident took place back in 1969, its impact was so great upon me that I still remember every detail. Here was the leader and founder of a successful international ministry graciously submitting to my immature leadership. I was deeply impressed and humbled at the same time. Not only did Loren give up the right of personal comfort to be with the team, he also encouraged my development as a fledgling leader by purposely putting himself in a place of submission to me for the duration of his stay. Loren's example at that point did more to shape my perspective on biblical leadership than any book I could have read or sermon I might have heard.

That which allows a leader to release people into their own ministry can be summed up in one word—*faith*. All leaders display faith in one form or another. Some place their faith in the quality of a training program. For others, it is faith in their own leadership ability. In both instances, the shallowness of faith will be exposed by the inability of the leader to trust those whom he releases. Faith always requires the extension of trust, but that trust must be in God, not in our ability, the trainees' ability, or the strength of our program.

The ability to extend trust to frail mortals displays the depth and quality of faith one has in God. Jesus, having great faith in his Father and demonstrating that faith by his obedience to the Father's will, placed more trust in the disciples than they would have placed in themselves.

The awe-inspiring greatness of Christ's splendor is defined not by the power of his natural attributes, but by the unfathomable depth of character he exhibited in entrusting the developing and equipping of his Church into the hands of mortal leaders...*and he does the same today!*

For Personal Study

1. What was my response when a leader placed trust in me? Was it a burden or a privilege?

2. Have I expected perfection from myself as a leader? From other leaders?

3. Have I ever betrayed the trust of someone who looked to me for leadership? What were the circumstances, and what can I learn from that situation?

4. Who are the people I really trust? Are they leaders, family members, friends? What have they done to gain my trust?

For Group Discussion

1. What qualified the disciples to become the apostles? Why do you think Jesus appointed the disciples to be apostles, even with their failings?

2. Why do you think God, who is perfect, trusts people, who are imperfect, with the responsibility of leading His Church?

3. Why can't trust be demanded? Can it be imparted? How?

4. Have you ever seen a leader release a younger leader into a leadership position and then change his mind? Discuss the effect this had on the younger leader.

CHAPTER TEN

Concluding Remarks

When speaking on servant leadership, more time has to be spent on describing the basic *attitudes* of a servant leader than on techniques or methods to employ when leading. This is because, generally speaking, if people develop the right attitudes, they will eventually do the right thing. Behavior normally follows attitude.

Further, there is no one style that defines servant leadership. Jesus employed a variety of techniques depending on the situation in which he found himself. Today, this is called *situational leadership*. A typical example is the concept of directing-coaching-delegating-releasing. Each of these modes is made to correlate to the needs and maturity of the person being led. It may be proper to use the coaching mode for one individual, the delegating mode for someone else. In other words, the leader tailors his style to the needs and maturity of the person he is leading.

Leadership style is also, at least to some degree, a matter of God-given personality and temperament. There is no personality that excludes a person from being a leader.

Neither is there any one type of personality that ensures that a person will become a leader. In today's world we often apply stereotypes to leadership roles. Thus, individuals with outgoing personalities are usually recognized as leadership material before introverts are seen as such.

Culture is yet another factor that can influence leadership style. In the Anglo-Saxon West, the tendency is to think that a take-charge style is the only way to lead. We find it easy to plunge ahead, assuming that the absence of immediate action within a group is an absence of leadership. Other cultures, however, are sometimes more discreet in style and see the West's eagerness to lead as a sign of arrogance. A leader friend of mine from Fiji once commented that his cultural tendency to extend courtesy before action was interpreted by Western leaders as lack of leadership ability. Yet, to apply Western boldness to island culture would prohibit any leadership influence from the Westerner.

The point is, leadership style is relative to a host of factors, including culture, personality, situation and maturity. Maybe that is why Jesus did not tell anyone how to be a leader in terms of methods to employ. Some who feel a potential calling to leadership are, therefore, often frustrated by Jesus' lack of clear teaching on this topic.

However, there are some critical ideas that have application to all cultures and personalities. For the sake of simplicity I call them Goal, Essence, Fuel, and Key Ingredients.

The Goal of Servant Leadership

The primary goal of a leader-trainer is to *grow people beyond himself*. Jesus said to the disciples that they would do even greater things than he did. This caused Jesus no feelings of insecurity. He genuinely wanted the disciples to become great leaders. Any good parent feels exactly the same in terms of training his or her own children. We who are parents hope that our kids will be better educated, have more money, and have greater influence than we. When our kids do well, we are their biggest cheerleaders.

We need to apply the same attitude of heart in the relationship of leader to trainee. True servant leaders know genuine joy when their former pupils grow beyond them. The younger leader is seen not as a threat but as the fruit of a job well done. The proof that a leader has been successful lies in the paradox that he is no longer needed.

The Essence of Servant Leadership

An old Chinese proverb says that a leader will know he has been successful when at the end of his leadership the people will say, "We did it ourselves." The quality hinted at in this proverb, and one that must lie at the heart of the true servant, is *hiddenness*. The servant leader is free from the noxious stipulation of ego that "I" must be seen. A favorite but rather obscure writer from the past, John Wright Follette, once said, "For ministry to truly be in the Spirit, the minister must be hidden."

While I cannot prove it from any one Scripture, I believe that in the cosmos that God created, the best leadership is that which *cannot* be seen. God is leading our own small planet toward a predetermined conclusion. As followers of Jesus, you and I know this to be true from the revelation of Scripture, as well as intuitively, yet we have a difficult time "seeing" God at work in his leadership role. Sometimes, like the Jewish nation of the Old Testament, we clamor for more visible leadership, leadership like the "Gentiles" have. That type of leadership is not what God intended. In the New Testament, it is even more obvious. When Jesus returned to heaven, *he left no single person in charge.* There was no "head apostle" appointed by Jesus. On a fallen planet, our need to know who's in charge is the very proof of our fallenness.

The Fuel of Servant Leadership

Given the above two concepts, it would be natural to ask, "How do you get anything done?" The answer is *inspiration*. True leaders have an ability to inspire others to greater accomplishment. This may be done through the power of example. Mother Theresa illustrates this point. Some leaders have an ability to inspire through their words. Winston Churchill used this ability during World War II. There are many ways to inspire and motivate without even holding a leadership position. Countless millions in India are still inspired by the life of Ghandi, who is no longer alive. The person who fails to inspire fails to lead.

When inspiration is missing, leaders must resort to force and command. Unfortunately, this way of leading now dominates (pun intended). Bribery, threats, and power become the tools used to get things done in the world's system. Thankfully, God never uses the implements of depraved man to accomplish anything in his Kingdom.

The Key Ingredients of Servant Leadership

Many ingredients must go into the mix for biblical leadership to emerge. They would include the fruit of the Spirit and the various spiritual gifts. Beyond these obvious characteristics, however, is another, often overlooked quality: the quality of *foresight*.[1] In terms of leadership, foresight is the ability to intuitively sense where things *ought* to go. It is a feeling for that which is not yet here. It is the gift that allows the servant to sense his master's requests before

> *Inspiration and genius—one and the same.*
>
> —*Victor Hugo*

---

1. This idea comes from one of my heroes, Tom Marshall. Mr. Marshall, recently deceased, was a quiet, gentle elder in the Body of Christ in New Zealand. The insight on foresight is to be found in his book, *Understanding Leadership*.

they are even verbalized. It is the ability of a leader to know in which direction to take those whom he is leading. The concept of leadership inherently implies direction and movement. There is no such thing as static leadership.

The servant leader is one who sees things about people that others often miss. He has a general sense about deployment of people's gifts and motivations and wants to see people fulfilled in their calling. He usually sees the danger points before others, and if not, he will know whom to call upon in avoiding potential pitfalls. He knows how critical it is to balance task accomplishment and personal development in the lives of those he serves.

A fascinating study was done a few years ago by British sociologist Elliot Jacques,[2] who wanted to know why some organizations sustained their viability over a long period of time. He concluded that a direct correlation exists between organizational viability and the foresight (or what Jacques called vision-span) of leadership. Short-lived organizations have an ability to see down the road a maximum of six months. Groups that maintain vitality over several generations are usually led by leaders who have a vision-span of fifty years. Clearly, foresight is indispensable to effective leadership.

> *To know that which before us lies in daily life, is the prime wisdom.*
>
> —*John Milton*

Synergy—The Power of the Team

A farmer once told me that a single horse hooked to a wagon can pull six tons. Two horses together can pull thirty-two tons. That is the power of synergy. Synergy is the concept that the whole is greater than the sum of its parts.

---

2. Dudley Lynch and Paul L. Kordis, *Strategy Of The Dolphin* (New York: Fawcett—Columbine, 1988), p.144-145.

Jesus understood the power of the team concept. He chose a team of twelve to establish his Church. In Luke 10, Jesus sent his followers out in teams of two. In the book of Acts we see teams of apostles moving in ministry together.

Today, teams of leaders are seen as a corporate invention used by innovative companies. But the concept of a team of leaders is timeless. Unfortunately, in recent Church history, examples of teams of leaders are the exception rather than the rule. Even where teams are attempted, it is usually the case that a senior leader heads up a team that functions more like a president and his cabinet than a true team.

In 1988, I was appointed North American Director of Youth With A Mission (YWAM). At the same time, I was serving as the local Seattle YWAM director. Since a number of other key YWAM leaders had also moved to Seattle, we felt it was important to meet and discuss our structure. What followed was a series of meetings in which together we developed a philosophy of team leadership. Our conclusion was that a team approach would work most effectively, given the makeup and responsibilities of the leaders involved. I was not *the leader* of that team. Here is the way we structured ourselves:

We were called the Leadership Council. Our job was to oversee the various ministries in the greater Seattle area. Here were the major components of our roles:

1. Every person had equal input into decision making.
2. The team delegated an individual to take responsibility for certain areas based upon ministry gift—e.g., those with visionary gifts were primarily responsible for the development of new ministries, and those with administrative gifts exercised their expertise on topics such as structure, finances, and policies.
3. A strong consensus was necessary for making decisions.
4. Different individuals chaired our meetings—there was no primary leader.
5. Each individual voluntarily agreed to be accountable to the group as a whole.

A common objection to team leadership is that "you still need someone to make the final decision." Our response was, *the team makes the final decision*. This never slowed us down or precluded us from making a decision. If a crucial decision was being made about *my* life and future, I would rather have a team of godly leaders with a variety of gifts and motivations make the decision than have one person make it.

Please bear in mind that leadership in the Old Testament was based upon a military format with a tight chain of command. Something changed under the New Covenant. John Stott says, "We need to remember that Jesus introduced into the world a new style of leadership, namely leadership by service and example, not by force."[3]

3. John Stott, *The Contemporary Christian*, (Downers Grove, IL, InterVarsity Press, 1992), p. 285.

Thus, in the New Testament, it is difficult to find whom people were "under." Whom was Paul under? How about Peter, or Barnabas? Was Barnabas in disobedience when he stood up to Paul regarding John Mark? Was Paul out of submission when he challenged Peter on the liberty of the gospel? After all, Peter held seniority in terms of years as an apostle. If Peter was a senior apostle, why did James give the summary statement in the dispute between Peter and Paul? Was James, therefore, the leader of the fledgling Church? The point is, no one person made the final decisions in the young Church. There are accounts of the apostles (plural) working as a team, deciding issues. This happened numerous times in the book of Acts.

Team leadership does *not* work unless team members have dealt with issues of control and ego. Any individual who has been used to "being in charge" will go through major adjustments. But when the team consists of servant leaders walking in reciprocal submission, the power of synergy kicks in. Creativity among team members begins to develop. Morale is elevated. When victories are won, the whole team shares the sense of satisfaction, but no one individual receives adulation. And, as it should be, only Jesus receives glory.

It's Time for a Revolution

For too long we in the Church have mixed ego with leadership. Larger-than-life heroes exist because we created them according to our own fantasies. When those same heroes prove to have feet of clay, we become suspicious and cynical. This is reflected in the attitudes of the American people, especially toward religious leaders. In a recent survey, Americans were asked to grade seventy-one professions for honesty and integrity. Catholic priests were the first religious leaders mentioned, at number seven. Jewish rabbis were ranked twelfth, and Protestant ministers came in at nineteenth. The lowest grades might be even more insightful: prostitutes ranked sixty-eighth; *television evangelists* were sixty-ninth. Organized crime bosses and drug dealers were the only professions ranked lower than television evangelists.[4] (Incidentally, firefighters were ranked number one.)

It is time for a new breed of leaders—both women and men—to emerge. These new leaders must be *real people*, full of integrity, not cutouts from a child's storybook. Listen to the discerning words of Oswald Chambers:

> Some of us want to be illuminated saints with golden halos and the flush of inspiration, and to have the saints of God dealing with us all the time. A gilt-edged saint is not good, he is abnormal, unfit for daily life, and altogether unlike God. We are here as men and women, not as half-fledged angels, to do the work of the world, and to do it with an infinitely greater power to stand the turmoil because we have been born from above.[5]

The shift from ego-centered leadership to servant leadership cannot be made unless God does a deep work of grace in our hearts. The events and changes taking place in the sanctuary of our souls determine the quality of service to those around us. Jesus-style leadership requires a personal commitment to serve others, regardless of the cost. The pilgrimage of the servant leader takes place beyond public view. Such a leader is the one who is willing to serve behind the scenes in that realm where no

4. James Patterson and Peter Kim, *The Day America Told The Truth* (New York: Prentice-Hall, 1991), pp. 142-143.

5. Oswald Chambers, *My Utmost For His Highest* (Uhrichsville, OH, Barbour and Co., 1963), p. 88.

public recognition can offer reward. Leadership of this type is not a grand spectacle conducive to hero worship and applause. It does, however, reflect the heart of the only true and perfect leader—Jesus. Learn from other leaders. Admire and respect them. But pattern yourself after only One!

❦

"A student is not above his teacher, nor a servant above his master. It is enough for the student to be like his teacher, and the servant like his master..."

—Jesus

For Personal Study

1. As a leader, have I been able to accomplish God-given ministry goals? Would the people I have led describe me as having the heart of a servant?

2. Am I locked into only one way of leading, or do I have the flexibility to lead according to the demands of the situation?

3. Have I honestly had a feeling of rejoicing when I have trained someone who has superseded me in ability and influence?

4. What have I done to foster synergy among those I lead? Am I a team player, or do I play only when I can be the boss?

5. Do I secretly cherish being seen as a leader, or am I willing to lead without taking credit?

For Group Discussion

1. Describe for the group the best team of which you have been a part. What made that particular team successful?

2. If you could put into one sentence the reason for servant leadership, what would it be?

3. When is it proper to be highly directive in leadership style? When does it not work?

4. When discussing team leadership, it is normally stated that someone has to have the final authority. The author seems to indicate that it is just as effective to have the team be the final authority. Discuss both sides of this issue. What are the strengths and weaknesses of each view?

COURAGEOUS LEADERS
Transforming Their World
   by James Halcomb, David Hamilton, and Howard Malmstadt, $15.99
Our world needs courageous leaders who will recognize the need for God-motivated action and follow through with a God-led plan. Whether your vision for change is local or global, simple or complex, for home, business, or ministry, *Courageous Leaders* will help you remain on a true course and reach the goal set before you.
(ISBN 1-57658-171-3)

WHY NOT WOMEN?
A Biblical Study of Women in Missions, Ministry, and Leadership
            by Loren Cunningham and David Hamilton, $14.99
Why Not Women? brings light, not just more heat, to the church's crucial debate with a detailed study of women in Scripture; historical and current global perspectives; an examination of the fruit of women in public ministry; and a hard-hitting revelation of what's at stake for women, men, the Body of Christ, God's Kingdom, and the unreached. (ISBN 1-57658-183-7)

IS THAT REALLY YOU, GOD?
Hearing the Voice of God
                        by Loren Cunningham, $9.99
This practical guide to hearing God's voice shows how an ordinary man who was committed to hearing God and obeying Him became the founder of the largest interdenominational missions organization in the world. (ISBN 0-927545-22-5)

MAKING JESUS LORD
The Dynamic Power of Laying Down Your Rights
                        by Loren Cunningham, $9.99
We live in a world in which the protection and exaltation of individual rights has become an obsession. As Christians we believe that personal rights do hold great value. As a result, we can perform no greater act of faith and worship than to consciously lay down these rights at the feet of the One who has gone before us, Jesus Himself!

Loren Cunningham details proven steps to a transformed life of freedom, joy, and intimate fellowship with God. Includes study guide. (ISBN 1-57658-012-1)

DARING TO LIVE ON THE EDGE
The Adventure of Faith and Finances

by Loren Cunningham, $9.99

Living by faith is not the domain of only those Christians called to "full-time" ministry. What is important is not our vocation, but whether we are committed to obeying God's will in our lives. If we are willing to step out in faith, doing whatever God has asked us to do, we will see His provision. A Christian who has experienced this is spoiled for the ordinary. (ISBN 0-927545-06-3)

SPIRITUAL WARFARE FOR EVERY CHRISTIAN
How to Live in Victory and Retake the Land

by Dean Sherman, $11.99

God has called Christians to overcome the world and drive back the forces of evil and darkness at work within it. Spiritual warfare isn't just casting out demons; it's Spirit-controlled thinking and attitudes. Dean delivers a no-nonsense, both-feet-planted-on-the-ground approach to the unseen world. Includes study guide. (ISBN 0-927545-05-5)

LOVE, SEX, AND RELATIONSHIPS

by Dean Sherman, $11.99

With clarity and a sharp wit, Dean Sherman illuminates the confusing and mysterious world of love, sex, and relationships in this accessible, hard-hitting examination of romantic love and sexuality in the Christian's life. Includes study guide. (ISBN 1-57658-141-1)

LEARNING TO LOVE PEOPLE YOU DON'T LIKE
How to Develop Love and Unity in Every Relationship

by Floyd McClung, $8.99

Does God really expect us to get along with each other? Floyd McClung offers challenging and practical answers for achieving productive, lasting relationships. Here is a firsthand account of how anyone can live in love and unity with others, both in the church and in the world. Includes study guide. (ISBN 0-927545-19-5)

FOLLOWING JESUS
Attaining the High Purposes of Discipleship

by Ross Tooley, $9.99

Following Jesus brings vision and direction to Christians who want to know God and make Him known. With straightforward teaching drawn from true stories of God's faithfulness and guidance, Ross Tooley examines how our passionate and patient God leads His present-day disciples into the dreams He has for them and for His Kingdom. (ISBN 1-57658-205-1)

DISCIPLING NATIONS
The Power of Truth to Transform Cultures

by Darrow Miller, $14.99

The power of the gospel to transform individual lives has been clearly evident throughout New Testament history. But what of the darkness and poverty that enslave entire cultures? In *Discipling Nations,* Darrow Miller builds a powerful and convincing thesis that God's truth not only breaks the spiritual bonds of sin and death but can free whole societies from deception and poverty. Excellent study of worldviews. Includes study guide. (ISBN 1-57658-015-6)

INTERCESSION, THRILLING AND FULFILLING

by Joy Dawson, $11.99

This book proves that we are surrounded by opportunities to impact our world through the powerful means of intercessory prayer. *Intercession, Thrilling and Fulfilling* spells out the price of obedience but leaves us in no doubt that the rewards and fulfillment far outweigh that price. We become history shapers and closer friends of Almighty God. (ISBN 1-57658-006-7)

INTERNATIONAL ADVENTURES
Amazing True Stories of Spiritual Victory and Personal Triumph

by various authors, $9.99 each

On every continent, in every nation, God is at work in and through the lives of believers. From the streets of Amsterdam to remote Pacific islands to the jungles of Ecuador and beyond, each international adventure that emerges is a dramatic episode that could be directed only by the hand of God...

Adventures in Naked Faith • ISBN 0-927545-90-X
Against All Odds • ISBN 0-927545-44-6
Dayuma: Life Under Waorani Spears • ISBN 0-927545-91-8
Imprisoned in Iran • ISBN 1-57658-180-2
Living on the Devil's Doorstep • ISBN 0-927545-45-4
The Man with the Bird on His Head • ISBN 1-57658-005-9
Tomorrow You Die • ISBN 0-927545-92-6
Torches of Joy • ISBN 0-927545-43-8
Totally Surrounded • ISBN 1-57658-165-9

CHRISTIAN HEROES: THEN AND NOW
Great missionary biographies for younger readers!

by Janet and Geoff Benge, $6.99 each
This popular series chronicles the exciting, challenging, and deeply touching true stories of ordinary men and women whose trust in God accomplished extraordinary exploits for His kingdom and glory. Real people—incredible, inspiring true stories for ages 10 and up.

Gladys Aylward • ISBN 1-57658-019-9
Corrie ten Boom • ISBN 1-57658-136-5
William Carey • ISBN 1-57658-147-0
Amy Carmichael • ISBN 1-57658-018-0
Loren Cunningham • ISBN 1-57658-199-3
Jim Elliot • ISBN 1-57658-146-2
Jonathan Goforth • ISBN 1-57658-174-8
Betty Greene • ISBN 1-57658-152-7
Adoniram Judson • ISBN 1-57658-161-6
Eric Liddell • ISBN 1-57658-137-3
David Livingstone • ISBN 1-57658-153-5
Lottie Moon • ISBN 1-57658-188-8
George Müller • ISBN 1-57658-145-4
Nate Saint • ISBN 1-57658-017-2
Mary Slessor • ISBN 1-57658-148-9
Hudson Taylor • ISBN 1-57658-016-4
Cameron Townsend • ISBN 1-57658-164-0

**Call 1-800-922-2143 for a full catalog,
or visit our website at www.ywampublishing.com**